S. HRG. 113–633

REGIONAL IMPLICATIONS OF A NUCLEAR DEAL WITH IRAN

HEARING

BEFORE THE

COMMITTEE ON FOREIGN RELATIONS UNITED STATES SENATE

ONE HUNDRED THIRTEENTH CONGRESS

SECOND SESSION

JUNE 12, 2014

Printed for the use of the Committee on Foreign Relations

Available via the World Wide Web: http://www.gpo.gov/fdsys/

U.S. GOVERNMENT PUBLISHING OFFICE

94–340 PDF   WASHINGTON : 2015

For sale by the Superintendent of Documents, U.S. Government Publishing Office
Internet: bookstore.gpo.gov   Phone: toll free (866) 512–1800; DC area (202) 512–1800
Fax: (202) 512–2104   Mail: Stop IDCC, Washington, DC 20402–0001

COMMITTEE ON FOREIGN RELATIONS

(II)

CONTENTS

(III)

REGIONAL IMPLICATIONS OF A NUCLEAR DEAL WITH IRAN

THURSDAY, JUNE 12, 2014

U.S. SENATE,
COMMITTEE ON FOREIGN RELATIONS,
Washington, DC.

The committee met, pursuant to notice, at 10 a.m., in room SD–419, Dirksen Senate Office Building, Hon. Robert Menendez (chairman of the committee) presiding.

Present: Senators Menendez, Cardin, Coons, Murphy, Kaine, Corker, Risch, Rubio, Johnson, Flake, Barrasso, and Paul.

OPENING STATEMENT OF HON. ROBERT MENENDEZ, U.S. SENATOR FROM NEW JERSEY

The CHAIRMAN. This hearing of the Senate Foreign Relations Committee will come to order.

Let me thank our panelists who I know will provide some thoughtful insights into the regional implications of a nuclear deal with Iran.

International attention is feverishly focused on the question of "if" the P5+1 and Iran will be able to agree and on what. I have strong views on what I think that agreement should look like and if we reach an agreement how we ensure Iranian compliance.

It is my view that any deal with Iran must demand significant dismantling of Iran's nuclear infrastructure, including eliminating the vast majority of Iran's centrifuge cascades and LEU's, which cannot mean leaving large stockpiles of LEU in oxide form that can easily be reconverted; terminating Iran's R&D efforts to create more advanced centrifuges; and fundamentally altering the internal infrastructure of the Arak facility, not just powering it down to a lower megawatt facility. Together, these elements must move the timeline for detectable breakout by Iran beyond a year.

Second, Iran must come clean and provide information about the military dimensions of its nuclear program and allow access to facilities where these activities have been taking place.

And third, the agreement must include a long-term robust inspections and verification regime, hopefully in the 20-year range, in other words, at least as long as Iran has been lying to the world about its program.

Fourth, any suspension of sanctions will require Iran to meet a series of clear benchmarks. There must be clear demarcations of what constitutes a breach, including implications for both nominal failure to comply and significant material breaches. Repercussions for a breach by Iran will be snapback provisions for sanctions. At

(1)

the end of the day, the specifics of the agreement will not be worth the paper they are written on if Iran believes it can cheat without significant repercussions.

Now, less attention is focused on perhaps the more critical, strategically relevant question: What happens after a deal? What are the strategic implications for the United States, for our allies and partners? What are the strategic implications of a politically and economically resurgent Iran, and what are the goals of its leaders in the aftermath of such a deal? I personally doubt that the nuclear deal is part of broader Iranian aspiration for a rapprochement with the United States.

This hearing will focus on what we should expect, how we should be preparing, and options we should be considering, if there is a deal. In other words, we must plan for a potential success. And in my view, success will not be defined exclusively by whether or not we get a good deal with Iran. The illicit nuclear program is only one pillar of much broader and equally troubling Iranian actions. Iranian support for terrorism goes back decades, and as we speak, Iran is actively cultivating terrorist networks and violent proxies across the region in Lebanon, Syria, Iraq, Bahrain, Yemen, the Palestinian territories, and beyond.

Our gulf partners are very concerned about Iran-sponsored terrorism. I heard this very clearly from Saudi and Emirati officials during my recent visit to the gulf. It is imperative that if we achieve a nuclear deal with Iran, our partners and allies are reassured that the United States remains committed to their security and is not naive about the nature of the Iranian threat and its hegemonic ambitions.

It is clear to me that our partners across the region are adopting hedging strategies toward Iran because United States commitment to the region is being actively questioned in light of our engagement with Iran and our hesitancy in Syria. This is evidenced by the string of Iranian official meetings and visits that has evolved from a trickle to a deluge. My concern is what will happen to gulf relationships with Iran after a deal is reached?

Finally, on sanctions, it is my view that the international sanctions regime has been the single most influential determinant in keeping the Iranians at the negotiating table. I look forward to hearing from our panelists on what the regional implications of sanctions relief would be. How will the Iranian Government use this potential economic windfall? Can we control access to those assets to ensure that they are not increasing their investment in regional destabilization?

At the end of the day, we must remain cognizant of Iranian motivations in pursuing a deal. Is it merely about sanctions relief for the leadership in Tehran, or is this about a broader realignment that could have serious strategic implications for the multidimensional chess game being played across the Middle East?

With that, let me recognize the distinguished ranking member of the committee, Senator Corker.

OPENING STATEMENT OF HON. BOB CORKER,
U.S. SENATOR FROM TENNESSEE

Senator CORKER. Thank you, Mr. Chairman, for having the hearing, and I want to thank our witnesses who always enlighten us. I know we have three very distinguished witnesses today.

I think, as the chairman mentioned, there is no question that there is a pretty major geopolitical shift that is occurring right now in the Middle East. The United States is facilitating that by the policies that we have not pursued or pursued, if you will, in Syria, by Iraq being weakened as it is, and Iran certainly playing a big role there. And our friends on the peninsula. I, too, was there recently and it is pretty amazing the shift in their attitude and the hedging that is beginning to take place there and the possibility, I might say, of tremendous amounts of proliferation should this arrangement, as it appears today, continue on.

I think all of us want to see a diplomatic solution. I do not think there is anybody on this dais that wants to see anything different from that. I think all of us have been pretty stunned, on the other hand, at the terms of the interim agreement and find it difficult for us to get to a good end state.

Candidly, some of the conversations we have privately with those involved in negotiations—some comments come out from time to time like, well, we really want to get them hooked on cash. In other words, we want them to see how well they can do with sanctions being undone and their economy growing and want relief even more so as to see this through.

So, look, again, I know we are at a critical period. I know there was a hastily called bilateral meeting that just took place. I have not had any readout as to whether it was successful or not. But there is no question that United States actions over the course of the last half a year, 9 months, have greatly strengthened Iran's role in the world. You know, even if we get a good deal, which I hope we do—that is the most important element, is to make sure that their program is dismantled, not mothballed. As they say, they can crank right back up in 30 days and be right back in business based on what they have been discussing with us today. I know all of us want to see a dismantlement so that that cannot occur.

But I want to emphasize again what the chairman has mentioned. Even if we make it through this successfully, which I hope with every cell of my body we do, they are still going to be a major state sponsor of terrorism. They are still going to be supporting a brutal dictator in Syria, and they are going to still be tremendous human rights violators.

So I thank you all for being here. I thank you for the wisdom you share. I look forward to your comments and our opportunity to follow up with questions. Thank you.

The CHAIRMAN. Thank you, Senator Corker.

Today we have a single panel of well-regarded experts. We are pleased to welcome Ambassador Dennis Ross, counselor and William Davidson Distinguished Fellow at the Washington Institute for Near East Policy; Scott Modell, senior associate and holder of the Burke Chair in Strategy at The Center for Strategic and International Studies; and Dr. Frederick Kagan, the Christopher

DeMuth chair and director of the Critical Threats Project at the American Enterprise Institute. Thank you all for being here.

Let me remind you that your full statements will be included for the record, without objection. I would ask you to try to summarize your statements in about 5 minutes or so, so that we can enter into a dialogue with you.

And with that, Ambassador Ross, we will start with you.

STATEMENT OF HON. DENNIS ROSS, WILLIAM DAVIDSON DISTINGUISHED FELLOW, COUNSELOR, THE WASHINGTON INSTITUTE FOR NEAR EAST POLICY, WASHINGTON, DC

Ambassador ROSS. Thank you, Mr. Chairman. It is a pleasure to be back here again before the committee.

I will summarize what I submitted to the committee.

I do want to start by saying I agree with your basic points on the essence of what a deal should be, and I do want to talk for a second about the deal not because I want to get into it but because I do not think right now the odds of reaching a deal are very high. It does not mean that it will never be achieved, but in the near term, I think it is not very likely.

I think what could make it likely is the Iranians seeing that the price is very high. Right now, the Iranian perception is that they do not have to roll back their program either because they do not believe they have to or because they are not prepared to. If we want to change that because they do, in fact, seek a rollback of sanctions, if we want to change their calculus, they have got to see that the failure of diplomacy is much worse for them than it is for us. They have got to see that the costs will go up dramatically for them not only economically, but even the huge investment they have made in their nuclear infrastructure could be lost if there is no diplomacy because there could well be military action.

The irony is the more we convey that kind of resolve, we make a deal more likely, but also the irony is the more we reassure our regional partners. The essence of this hearing is supposed to be about the implications of a deal, and the fact is today, if there were a deal, it would cause great concern among both our regional partners, meaning Arab partners but also Israel, but for different reasons.

The Saudis, in particular—the Emiratis you mentioned you have just seen them. They look at themselves as being engaged in an existential struggle right now with Iran not because of the nuclear issue. They view the nuclear issue as being an instrument in what is an Iranian effort to gain regional dominance.

From a Saudi perspective, what do they see in the region right now? They see troubles in their eastern province. They see Bahrain. They see Iraq. They see Syria. They see Lebanon. They see Yemen. Everywhere they see an Iranian hand. And that they view as an existential struggle. So if, in fact, there were a deal, from their standpoint right now, the deal would either provide a kind of license to the Iranians to do much more, but would also provide them the wherewithal to do much more. They would be out from under severe economic sanctions. They would be freed of that. They view the deal itself as being a function of our desire, an American desire, whether their perception is right or not—and I think their perception, by the way, is exaggerated, but their perception exists. And that perception is basically our concern with the nuclear issue trumps everything else.

Now, that is a view that is also shared by the Israelis, but their point of departure is different. They view the Iranian behavior in the region as a problem but one they can deal with. They view the nuclear issue as an existential threat. A deal from the Israeli standpoint would be fine if it does not leave the Iranians as a threshold nuclear state where, at a time of their own choosing, they could end up breaking out.

So how to deal with these collective set of concerns that exist about Iran but are not entirely motivated by the same factors. I am going to suggest to you a few things that we could be doing that would be appropriate for both sets of concerns, on the one hand, but I will also offer a few tailored ideas on the other.

What is the most important factor for us? We need to demonstrate unmistakably that we are prepared to compete with the Iranians. And I would identify two things we could do that would have an impact on both our key Arab friends and the Israelis. Syria. You mentioned Syria. The more we are seen as being prepared to compete there, meaning we are prepared to raise the price to the Iranians of what they are doing in Syria. We are prepared to change the balance of power on the ground, meaning not only between those in the opposition vis-a-vis ISIS, who is obviously a source of concern, given what is going on in Iraq now, but also vis-a-vis the regime in Syria, Bashar al-Assad regime, where the Iranians are all in with them.

Now, what does that mean in practical terms? It does not mean boots on the ground. It does mean the United States being prepared to quarterback the effort to provide meaningful assistance, including lethal assistance, designed to affect the balance of power on the ground. It means having the United States work with everybody else who is providing assistance, making sure that it is coordinated, it is complementary, it is additive, and in fact, it goes and addresses the purpose that we seek. That is one thing that we could do.

A second thing we could do is we could actively interdict the Iranian and clandestine arms shipments around the region. When the Israelis interdicted the *Klos C* shipment that was going from Iran taking Iranian arms to Gaza, had we done that, the impact on the region and the impact on the Iranians would have been big. For those who feel that, gee, that might threaten what we are doing with Iran, Iran does not seem to have a problem negotiating with us on the nuclear issue and being very active throughout the region at the same time. There is absolutely no reason that we cannot do the same thing with them.

And by the way, if what you are trying to do is to enhance Rouhani's position, you do not enhance Rouhani's position by showing that Qasem Soleimani is able to do things that do not cost the Iranians. It is the IRGC al-Quds Brigade that is active throughout the region, and we need to show that there is a cost to the Iranians for doing this, not only showing them that there is a cost to do something else, it would also have the benefit of reassuring our friends in the region that we mean what we say. We have resolve.

We are not turning a blind eye to what the Iranians are doing in the region to change the regional balance of power. We are prepared to compete with them.

I know my time is about up. So let me cite a few other things we could be doing that is tailored more specifically to each side, to what the Saudi concerns could be, as an example, what the Israelis' concerns could be for an example.

I will give you just one example on the Saudis. There is a series of things that we could do with the Saudis, the Emiratis, and others, but just one thing that would make a big difference with the Saudis and the Emiratis. How about doing contingency planning? How about sitting down with them and saying let us look at the array of threats that we see throughout the region that are coming from the Iranians. We are not just going to do an assessment of them. Let us do contingency planning with you so that we could actually counter them, be prepared for them, deal with them. The signal that would send to each of them would be, I think, quite remarkable at this point.

And again, one of the reasons you want to do this is it gets at what both the chairman and Mr. Corker were saying. We do not want them going off on their own and in a sense either engaging in hedging strategies or doing other things where the Saudis go ahead and they parade Chinese missiles. They are doing that for a reason, and it is sending a message to us and to others in the region. We want them to be more reassured about us. So contingency planning with the Saudis and the Emiratis I think would go a long way toward addressing concerns that they have.

With the Israelis, I will give you two examples of things that we could do.

If the big Israeli fear is that you have a deal that could allow the Iranians to break out or to creep out, then one of the things you have to do with the Israelis is to give them a high level of assurance that we are very well focused on how the Iranians could cheat, and more importantly, we are very well focused on making sure there is a severe consequence for cheating. We should be talking to the Israelis about identifying where they could break out, where the Iranians could break out or creep out if there is an agreement. We should be focused on what the cheating could look like. We should talk with the Israelis about what we are prepared to do, realizing that if we can do it collectively, it is one thing internationally, but being prepared to do things on our own if that is not the case. And that is not just economically. It might also have to involve the use of force under certain circumstances.

The second thing we could do with the Israelis, because they might still fear that for whatever reasons we might constrain ourselves in the event of a violation, which after all, if you look at the history of arms control agreements, it is not exactly unusual for there to be violations of arms control agreements—one of the things we could do with the Israelis is make it clear to them that we would support what they would do. We could have conversations with them, identify categories of different kinds of violations of the agreement, and the more extreme the violations, we could be prepared to support what the Israelis' actions would be, and that could even involve us providing the Israelis, in the event of an agreement, certain forms of compensation that could include the provision of capabilities that the Israelis themselves do not have today that could be useful for them if they had to act militarily. Sending that message not only to the Israelis but others in the region, including the Iranians, I think again ironically would reinforce the larger purpose of reaching an agreement in the first place, but if we do reach that agreement, then dealing with some of the concerns that you raised in your opening statement.

Thank you.

[The prepared statement of Ambassador Ross follows:]

PREPARED STATEMENT OF AMBASSADOR DENNIS ROSS

America's readiness to negotiate a deal with the Islamic Republic on its nuclear program is a source of deep concern among our traditional friends in the Middle East. For the Arabs, the fear is that the deal will come at their expense, with the United States increasingly seeing Iran as a partner. For the Israelis, the worry is that we will conclude a deal that leaves the Iranians as a threshold nuclear state—capable of breaking out to nuclear weapons at a time when we might be distracted by another international crisis.

Both sets of fears presume that there will be a deal. While the committee has asked us to discuss the regional implications of such a deal, I should note at the outset that I still believe the prospects of an agreement are probably less than the 50-percent figure President Obama cited late last year. Basic conceptual gaps remain, with the Iranians still believing that their limited offers of transparency should be sufficient to satisfy our concerns about the peaceful character of their nuclear program. Will the Supreme Leader, who has talked about not dismantling their program, accept a serious reduction in the numbers of their centrifuges? We will see, but at this point, Ali Khamenei either is not prepared to roll back Iran's nuclear program or doesn't believe he will have to do so in order to produce a serious rollback in the sanctions regime. He does not appear to understand that there can be no rollback in sanctions without a rollback and deep reduction in the Iranian nuclear program—meaning Iranian centrifuges must be dramatically reduced in number; much of the accumulated enriched uranium must be shipped out of the country; Fordow must be shut down or completely disabled; and the Arak heavy water plant must be converted so it cannot produce plutonium.

The Iranian negotiators at this point have given no indication of being able to accept such a rollback. And yet, if we are to concede limited enrichment for the Iranians, rollback of this sort plus transparency both beyond the Additional Protocol and about the possible military dimensions of their program will be required. Even if President Rouhani and Mohammad Javad Zarif, his foreign minister, are ready to accept such a deal—and it is not clear that they are—can they sell this to the Supreme Leader? Maybe, but I suspect that still remains a long shot.

To be sure, if there is to be a deal, the Supreme Leader must see the very high costs to the Islamic Republic of diplomacy failing. He must be convinced that such failure will mean enduring, severe economic pain for Iran as well as the high probability that force will be used to destroy the huge investment the Islamic Republic has made in its nuclear facilities. Ironically, that posture—which may make a deal more likely—would also be useful for assuaging the deep concerns our regional friends have about any possible P5+1 nuclear accord with the Iranians.

Both the Israelis and our key Arab friends believe that we are anxious for a nuclear deal, and they are not taking seriously the administration's declarations that no deal would be better than a bad deal. They see active Iranian efforts to change the balance of power in the region and, fairly or not, little sign that we are prepared to compete with the Iranians as they do so. That has led to a perception among our regional friends that we attach such importance to a deal on the Iranian nuclear program that we turn a blind eye to Iranian behavior in the region.

The administration argument that it is simply separating the nuclear issue from the other Iranian challenges in the area has not altered the impression of many in the region that our concerns about the Iranian nuclear program trump everything else. Here, it is worth highlighting that the Israeli and Arab concerns are different when it comes to Iran.

For the Israelis, their priority is the Iranian nuclear program. That constitutes an existential threat. Iran and its proxies like Hezbollah constitute a threat, but, in Israeli eyes, that is manageable. Iran possessing nuclear weapons is not manageable or containable. For the Saudis, Iran already represents an existential threat even without nuclear weapons. The Saudis, Emiratis, and others see an aggressive Iranian pursuit of regional hegemony. From a Saudi standpoint, the Iranians are encircling them—seeking to gain dominance in, and the ability to threaten them overtly and covertly from, Bahrain, Iraq, Syria, Lebanon, and Yemen. The Iranian nuclear program would add to the threat—perhaps making the Iranians less risk averse—but it is not the source of the problem they see.

Talk of a possible reconciliation between Saudi Arabia and Iran is likely to mean little. They are competitors in every sense of the word. It is not just Arab versus Persian, Sunni versus Shiite, or even traditional balance of power concerns related to regional dominance. It is all of these things, and it goes to the source of legitimacy for each. The Islamic Republic challenges the legitimacy of any monarchy and has pretensions to lead Muslims internationally. The Saudis see a fundamental threat to their role in leading Sunnis and feel that Iran challenges it religiously.

For the Saudis, an Iran with nuclear weapons requires a countervailing response; such weapons would certainly add to the dangers. But in the near term, the Saudis may fear even more an Iran that is no longer being damaged by severe economic sanctions, no longer isolated internationally, increasingly able to develop economically, and with more means for troublemaking. As such, the Saudis, in particular, may fear that a deal on the nuclear program will not only signal a new American openness to Iran, but, even more, give the Iranians license to be more aggressive in the region, and with the economic wherewithal to do so. Words alone will not reassure the Saudis in the aftermath of a deal. They will look for signs that a nuclear deal is not going to transform our relationship with Iran—and that we will be vigilant in countering Iran's threats in the area.

Unlike the Saudis, the measure for the Israelis is what kind of deal is reached. The Saudis will be suspicious of any nuclear deal; for the Israelis, it depends on the deal. A deal that precludes the Iranians from being able to turn a civil nuclear program into a nuclear weapons capability would be welcomed. Such a deal would remove an existential threat to Israel. The problem for the Israelis is that the deal that would make them most comfortable is probably not attainable in the P5+1 negotiations; Israelis feel that Iran must be denied an ongoing enrichment capability. While that would be for the best from a strictly nonproliferation standpoint, it is probably not attainable—at least that is the consensus of those members of the P5+1 negotiating with the Iranians. The question for the Israelis becomes whether they can be reassured enough about the scope of the rollback of the Iranian program, the transparency measures designed to prevent cheating on the rollback, and the credible consequences that would be imposed on the Iranians if they cheated anyway.

What implications does this have for our approach toward our regional friends if there is a deal? Since the Saudi and Israeli concerns are different, our approaches to them should also differ in some respects. That said, anything which suggests that the United States will actively compete with the Iranians would be reassuring to both. All of our friends want to see that we will not permit Iran to become stronger in the region at their expense, that we will be there for our friends if they face threats, and that we don't so fear conflict with Iran that we will acquiesce to any of its behaviors.

In this regard, there are two steps we could take that would be reassuring to Arabs and Israelis alike:

- Demonstrate in Syria that our concern is about both the growth of the jihadist presence in the country and the prospects of Assad cementing his hold on power. The former threatens all of us; the latter would signal a victory for Iran and the demonstration that it succeeds when it uses its power to alter the landscape in the region. We need to show that we will not acquiesce to that outcome. This means not just increasing lethal assistance to the pragmatic Syrian opposition, but doing so with an eye toward changing the balance of power on the ground, including between the opposition and the regime. This means taking control of the collective effort to support the opposition—through training, material assistance, arming, etc.—in order to make sure that everything that is being done to support the acceptable opposition is coordinated and complementary.
- Show that we will not allow the Iranians to ship arms clandestinely around the region. This means interdicting clandestine Iranian arms shipments. The Israelis interdicted the *Klos C* ship carrying Iranian arms to Gaza, but we should have done it. We don't have to announce what we are doing or even take public credit for it; we just need to do it. The Iranians and our friends will see it and understand that we are competing and that the Iranians will pay a price for what they are doing.

As for additional steps geared toward the specific concerns of Arabs and Israelis, we might launch contingency planning with the Saudis and Emiratis on how we would deal with particular Iranian threats. This would show our seriousness and also put us in a position to act when needed; if this meant different kinds of exercises with each, the Iranians would also get the message.

With the Israelis, if there is a nuclear deal, we could discuss the specific steps we would take if the Iranians cheat on a deal and how we would impose consequences—even anticipating that there might be reluctance on the part of others to hesitate in the face of violations of the agreement. We might also compensate the Israelis if there is a deal by providing more bunker-buster bombs and more tankers to make them more capable of militarily acting on their own against the Iranians in the face of cheating. This would reassure the Israelis that even if we felt constrained to act militarily in the face of Iranian violations of an agreement that made a breakout possible, Israel would not be left without options.

CONCLUSIONS

Our traditional friends in the Middle East are very suspicious about Iran's aims in the region. Although the Obama administration has tried to reassure the Saudis, Emiratis, and Israelis about our commitments and our understanding of Iranian behavior, there are deep-seated doubts about what we are actually prepared to do. While our hesitancy on Syria may reflect understandable concerns about avoiding a quagmire, the Iranians show no such hesitancy and have invested heavily in ensuring the survival of the Assad regime. In a region where an Iranian win is seen as a loss for our friends, the worries about us have increased. It is through that lens that many of our regional friends view a possible nuclear deal with Iran. The Israeli and Saudi fears are different, but if we want to reassure our friends about such a deal, we need to understand the source of their worries and take steps that address them. That does not mean accepting fears that we think are misplaced, but it does mean taking steps that can make us more secure and also signal to the Iranians they will pay a price for behaviors outside the nuclear area that we find unacceptable. Ironically, that may make a deal itself more likely.

The CHAIRMAN. Thank you.
Mr. Modell.

STATEMENT OF SCOTT MODELL, SENIOR ASSOCIATE, BURKE CHAIR IN STRATEGY, CENTER FOR STRATEGIC AND INTERNATIONAL STUDIES, WASHINGTON, DC

Mr. MODELL. Chairman Menendez, Ranking Member Corker, thank you for the opportunity.

I would like to talk a little bit about my background before I get into my comments because it sort of colors what observations I want to make today.

Prior to joining CSIS, I was in the Central Intelligence Agency, the Director of Operations, did five tours overseas. On my last tour, I oversaw Iranian operations there, Iranian internal operations, and oversaw a lot of the global external operations against the Iran threat network. So much of what I am going to say today has to do with observations on the basis of that experience that go into my thoughts on how the Iran threat network has evolved over the last 5 years, and in the aftermath of the nuclear deal, good or bad, how that Iran threat network is going to continue to be a problem for us.

I would like to start with 2009 and the Green Movement. In 2009, as the Green Movement began to coalesce and the Supreme Leader finally came around to understanding that it was a problem—it was an existential threat for the Iranian Government—they realized they had to dismantle it piece by piece, and they cleared out Evin Prison and they decided that they did not want to make the same mistake that the Shah had made in the late 1970s. And it is exactly what they did. They went and they dismantled it, and it had a profound effect on the Iran threat network. The internal security apparatus got better. The MOIS, the IRGC, the law enforcement forces, the Basij, everybody came together in ways that they had not come together before.

Fast forward to a year or so later when they were faced with attacks on their nuclear facilities. The presence of Stuxnet led to some unintended consequences, led to strengthening of their nuclear facilities, their industrial security, their cyber security, their ability to detect personnel that were not deemed sufficiently wedded to the revolution, and it sort of strengthened the internal security apparatus, as well as their apparatus overseas, the Iran threat network.

Fast forward to 2012 and 2013. The sanctions regime that was put into place against Iran—when the United States and the European Union initially went through with an oil embargo, the Iranian Supreme Leader had come to the conclusion that the price of oil was going to increase from about $100 a barrel to $200 barrel and thought that it would be unsustainable for the world. When that did not happen, he realized that they had to come to the table and negotiate. So I agree with the comments made by the chairman initially that the only reason that they are negotiating right now is because there was a collapse of the economy and that economic recovery was a must for them.

I think the fundamental strategic calculus of the Supreme Leader remains the same. It is preservation of the regime at home. And they have broader regional goals that they are going to continue to push.

Now, as far as a nuclear deal, I think there is going to be a nuclear deal. I do not think it is going to be a good deal. I think it is going to go on. I think there are going to be several phases to it. I think that it is going to be presented as a fait accompli to the international community. It is something we are going to have to accept and for several years try to figure out what it is going to look like and how to implement it. And I think, like Mr. Ross said, as it frees up money for the Iranian Government, it is only going to embolden the Iran threat network even further.

As far as solutions, one of the things I have seen in the way that the U.S. Government is postured toward dealing with the Iran threat network—I think there are a number of things that we have already done that we can take advantage of particularly on the law enforcement side. I think in the presence of sanctions that are eased and the presence of credible war options being taken off the table, I think there needs to be more of a focus on law enforcement. I think that the Department of the Treasury needs to start looking closer at overseas financial operations. I think we need to start looking at counterthreat facilitation which would be going after the criminal networks that the Iran threat network has built up over the last couple of years in order to evade sanctions. I think that network is going to go on in the aftermath of a nuclear agreement. And I think having a better understanding about how Iran evades sanctions, their transportation networks, their intelligence networks, the way they move men, money, and material around the world, that feeds right into the necessity of coming up with a comprehensive compliance and verification mechanism, which I think will be extremely difficult.

Like the chairman mentioned, we need at least two decades of figuring out if Iran is going to be an honest nuclear broker. For us to figure out just the military dimensions of that program, it is going to take quite a bit of time. I think figuring out how to use our law enforcement overseas to detect cheating is something critical that we will have to continue to focus on.

In the case of Treasury, for instance, the Department of the Treasury has done a fantastic job over the years of collecting information on individuals, groups, and entities that are involved in the proliferation of sanctioned materials. We need to do a better job of working with foreign liaison partners to actually take advantage of that. There are a number of things we could be doing government-wide to take advantage of the information we have, and working with our allies to do more against the Iran threat network.

As far as regional implications, as far as the GCC goes, I tend to agree I think they are shocked at what has transpired. And they are looking for answers and they are looking for reassurance. But I would also say that I tend to think that the bilateral security relationships between the United States and our gulf allies is strong. It is very strong. I think that they are beginning to contemplate things they had not contemplated in the past. But, nevertheless, I think the lack of alternatives for them, in terms of greater security arrangements, is going to force them to continue to rely on the United States.

I think we should be very cautious when we hear statements from Saudi leaders and other gulf countries talking about the formation of joint military commands and GCC-specific entities that are trying to enhance interoperability and jointness. They have been talking about that for a long time. I think they are starting to talk about it again on the basis of perceived weakness on our part. But I think there is enough reassurance and I think there is enough long-standing faith in the bilateral relationships we have in terms of security to keep those relationships going.

I would argue that what is going on in Iraq is going to be particularly troubling. Soleimani I think is going to see that as an opportunity to actually do what he has not been able to do over the last couple of years due to budgetary constraints. New units are going come online. New proxies are going to be more deeply funded, and I think you are going to see a much more active Quds Force inside of Iraq.

I think the same thing with Syria. As well as they have done in Syria in creating basically a nationwide Basij force for the Syrians, I think that is going to go on. They are going to look to make that permanent in Syria. I think the idea of the Shia crescent—there is truth to that, and they are going to continue to find ways to build on that.

As far as regional implications of sort of an embolden Iran, I think when you look at their efforts further out in places like Latin America and Africa, I would give it a mixed review in terms of success. They have had a very difficult time establishing a foothold in places like Latin America. They have had to downsize recently because of budgetary constraints, but nevertheless, they are pushing intel officers and military attachés and new embassies into the region. They are doing what they can. But again, there is not as much receptivity in that part of the world as they would like. So I think they are going to continue to focus on their part of the world.

So the regional implications of a nuclear deal and the influx of cash will be, I think, a near-term sort of up-tick in their operations within the Iran threat network.

[The prepared statement of Mr. Modell follows:]

PREPARED STATEMENT OF SCOTT MODELL

June 12, 2014 Chairman Menendez, Ranking Member Corker, members of the committee, good afternoon and thank you for this opportunity to testify on the regional implications of a nuclear agreement with Iran. I will briefly describe the mind-set of Iran's Supreme Leader and the Iran Threat Network, list some of the regional implications of a nuclear deal between Iran and the P5+1 countries, and offer recommendations for the administration and Congress on future efforts to counter one of our most pressing national security challenges.

REVOLUTION, RESISTANCE, AND THE SUPREME LEADER

After the 1979 Islamic Revolution, Iran set out to radically change its posture toward all nations, especially the United States. For the last 35 years it has kept its word, sponsoring terrorism, deceiving the international community about its nuclear program, supporting violent proxies against U.S. interests around the world, and above all, building a multifaceted global apparatus—political, ideological, religious, and criminal—to pursue a revolutionary agenda that envisions a new balance of power in the world.

The Supreme Leader has consistently referred to "resistance" when describing Iran's struggle with the West, similar to the way Americans speak of freedom—as a nonnegotiable value and source of national pride. The concept of resistance is critical for understanding why the Supreme Leader continues to champion Iran's role as the leader of an "Axis of Resistance" and openly condemn U.S. values, character, and foreign policy. It lies at the core of his strategic calculus and drives the pursuit of two fundamental goals: preserving the regime at home and promoting the revolution abroad.

Khamenei begrudgingly supports the P5+1 nuclear talks, skeptical that the United States will follow through on the terms of any deal. He recognizes, however, that a deal is necessary to ease the pressure of economic sanctions and revive Iran's economy, but will not allow a deal to become the gateway to U.S.-Iran rapprochement. As Foreign Minister Zarif has stated, "Iran is looking for common ground, not friendship."

The Supreme Leader's closest advisors, such as Deputy Chief of Staff Asghar Mir-Hejazi, former IRGC commander and military advisor Yahya Rahim Safavi, and Supreme Council for National Security Chairman Ali Shamkhani have explained that severe budget cuts have had negative impact on the ability of Iran to conduct overseas operations. This has taken a particularly heavy toll on the IRGC Quds Force, which has the largest role in Iran's external resistance mission.

THE IRAN THREAT NETWORK

The Iran Threat Network is the global apparatus that Iran has used for more than three decades to promote the goals of the Islamic Revolution. It consists of a network of government and nongovernmental organizations that are involved in crafting and implementing the covert elements of Iran's foreign policy agenda, from terrorism, political, economic, and social subversion; to illicit finance and weapons trafficking; and nuclear procurement and proliferation. Iran relies primarily on three organizations to coordinate and oversee the activities of the Iran Threat Network:

- The Quds Force, an elite branch of the Islamic Revolutionary Guard Corps, responsible for irregular warfare and asymmetric operations, including a wide range of subversive activities from nonviolent cultural and business fronts to direct support to political resistance organizations and violent opposition groups.
- The Ministry of Intelligence and Security (MOIS) is Iran's primary civilian intelligence agency. It has the lead role in foreign intelligence collection and

several covert action programs, both at home and abroad. It works closely with all of Iran's closest proxies in the region and second only to the Quds Force in Iran's global efforts to export the Islamic Revolution.

- Lebanese Hezbollah has been Iran's strongest nonstate ally since its inception in 1982. While Hezbollah's role in projecting Iranian power has traditionally been tied to the goals of fighting Israel and protecting Lebanon, it remains a key element in fighting on the front lines in Syria, alongside Quds Force advisors and trainers and Syrian army units.

The Iran Threat Network is Iran's "whole-of-government" approach to preserving the regime at home and coordinating and promoting the revolution internationally. Its actions encompass a remarkable array of covert action, including covert influence operations, sanctions evasion, terrorism, training and equipping Islamic militants, and other so-called "resistance activities."

THE REGIONAL IMPLICATIONS OF A NUCLEAR DEAL

Weak or strong, comprehensive or limited, any deal will take several years if not decades to implement. In many countries of the region, the status quo will make way for a nuclear Iran. No countries, rhetoric aside, supports preemptive strikes against Iranian nuclear sites unless there is overwhelming evidence of further Iranian deception. Iran will be under tremendous pressure to comply with a comprehensive agreement, but has no apparent intention of slowing down its drive to achieve broader regional goals, which often conflicts with U.S. and allied security interests. If a deal is reached, there are several implications to keep in mind:

- First, an agreement will give a much-needed boost to the Iranian economy. By most accounts, Iran stands to gain access to nearly $100 billion frozen in foreign banks, as well as billions more as oil export restrictions are lifted. At the same time, several EU countries appear poised to return to Iranian markets, adding billions of dollars more in potential foreign direct investment and trade. All of this will provide the leaders of the Iran Threat Network with the resources they need to gradually return to previous levels of operational activity. It means funding proxies that were either cut off or cut back due to sanctions; reassessing the ongoing closure or downsizing of Iranian embassies in nontraditional areas such as Latin America; expanding joint military training and security programs in Africa; and increasing funding for HAMAS, PIJ, and the new Palestinian coalition government.
- Second, several countries in the gulf should expect to see a resumption of covert activity, including training, weapons, and nonlethal support to local proxies, especially in Bahrain, Kuwait, and Saudi Arabia, where Iran has a history of supporting Shia opposition movements. The GCC countries will also have to confront the growing threats posed by Iran in the area of Computer Network Exploitation operations. Iranian hackers employed primarily by the MOIS target the computer systems of U.S. and gulf personnel, companies, and government facilities. Iran has treated past Stuxnet attacks on centrifuges at Natanz as a declaration of cyber war, and is now responding in kind.
- Third, IRGC Quds Force Commander Qasem Soleimani will find ways of increasing military support to the Assad regime. Keeping Assad in power will remain a strategic priority, mainly because it strengthens Iran's relationship with its most important partner in the region, Lebanese Hezbollah, but also because in Iran's eyes there is no alternative. Soleimani will also be focused on countering the growth of Sunni extremism in Iraq, which has reached levels of violence unseen since 2007. He will probably offer to increase current initiatives that arm, train, and fund new and existing pro-Iranian Shia militants in Iraq. Soleimani has more say over what Iran does in Syria and Iraq than President Rouhani, enjoying the full support of the Supreme Leader. His number one priority will remain building an arc of influence and power across the Levant, often referred to as Iran's "Shia crescent."
- Fourth, there are few signs that a nuclear Iran will increase the chances of a near-term nuclear arms race in the Middle East. U.S.–GCC bilateral security relationships have evolved for more than 25 years. Any strategic shift away from the United States would take years given the depth of the commitments involved. GCC countries are rightfully more concerned about Iran's attempts to exploit the very real issues of religious extremism, demographic pressures, and other internal sources of instability that each Gulf State is trying to address on its own.
- Fifth, Iran has gone to considerable lengths to create a global shadow apparatus designed to evade sanctions. It enables the Iranian Government to support Islamic movements and pro-Iran militants around the world and spread the

value of the "resistance" via cultural, social, economic, political, and business entities and organizations. That apparatus goes hand in hand with the asymmetrical nature of almost everything it does. The international community needs to develop a better understanding of this apparatus for several reasons, but largely because it is directly linked to some of Iran's most destabilizing activities.

- Sixth, as long as a nuclear deal does not address Iran's ballistic missile program, which appears to be the case given outright rejection of the idea by the Supreme Leader, Iran will continue to develop long-range ballistic missiles that can strike any target in the GCC and add further to its arsenal of short-range artillery rockets that can strike coastal areas across the gulf. Iran will attempt to improve the accuracy of its missiles and rockets, and pursue the indigenous production of UCAVs, cruise missiles, and possibly even nuclear warheads.

THE WAY FORWARD

Even if sanctions and diplomacy lead to a nuclear agreement with Iran, the activities of the Iran Threat Network will continue to pose significant obstacles to Iran's diplomatic outreach to the gulf and the West. In some cases, lethal support to Shia opposition groups across the region also threatens both U.S. and international security. To address these threats, policymakers should consider the following recommendations:

- *Coordinate U.S. Efforts Against Networks.* U.S. policymakers should call for an interagency and international task force for developing and deploying a comprehensive and global campaign against the operational and strategic depth of the Iran Threat Network. Such a task force would target the illicit networks and operatives associated with the Iran Threat Network, including its financial, business, and logistical support networks. The goal should be a counter network disruption campaign, modeled where appropriate, on previous successful U.S. whole-of-government initiatives against defiant state actors that combine overt and covert action, law enforcement, sanctions, and containment.
- *Refine and Expand Soft War Initiatives.* The Supreme Leader repeatedly refers to the U.S.-led "soft war" as the single biggest threat to the existence of the Islamic Republic. An effective soft war should expose and neutralize the state and nonstate actors involved in subversive activities that are instrumental in marketing the Islamic Revolution overseas. At the very least, this should include Quds Force, MOIS, and Hezbollah operations and criminal activities. Of equal importance are Iran's nonofficial cover organizations—religious, cultural, and charitable—as well as businesses that effectively blur the lines between overt and covert activity.
- *Focus Efforts on Transnational Organized Crime.* In addition to being one of the world's most formidable terrorist and paramilitary organizations, Hezbollah has become involved in a global criminal enterprise involving money laundering, racketeering, and drug trafficking. Indicting Hezbollah as a transnational criminal organization would dispel its image as an elite and "pure" resistance organization. We should approach and counter Hezbollah from the vantage point of strategic law enforcement, financial sanctions, and even the International Court of Criminal Justice (for its long record of global terrorism, for its involvement in the assassination of a democratically elected head of state, and possibly even for war crimes being perpetrated in Syria).
- *Developing Nonmilitary Policy Options.* At any given time, dozens of U.S. Government agencies are pursuing the same elements of the Iran Threat Network. To improve the way multiple agencies work against the Iran Threat Network, the government has to be better organized. In relatively new and developing areas such as Counter Threat Finance, it would go a long way to work from an agreed-upon "financial order of battle" that maps key networks on a transnational scale (e.g., banks, exchange houses, front companies, trade-based money laundering, shipping companies, etc.). In doing so, U.S. Government agencies should draw assiduously on partner country liaison services as part of a global effort to build a coalition of like-minded states. An order of battle would generate a series of nonmilitary or military-enabled policy options that could serve as the basis of a strategic intelligence and law enforcement campaign—not just a series of strikes.
- *Focus on Counter Threat Facilitation.* As long as Iran has an agenda of creating new centers of power in the world and doing so at the expense of the United States, it behooves us to consider a law enforcement-led "Counter Threat Facilitation" initiative. Such an initiative should emphasize strategically planned law enforcement operations to expose illicit networks, arrest their perpetrators,

freeze assets and attack the Iran Threat Network's crime-terror pipelines though the international trade and banking system. It could go a long way in weakening the illicit financial networks around the world that buttress Iran's strategic foundations, revolutionary resolve, domestic staying power, and power projection capabilities.

- *Create Offices of Irregular Warfare.* As sanctions are eased, the U.S. Government will need to find other ways of identifying and disrupting Iran's involvement in nuclear proliferation, terrorism, and other threats to international security. If sanctions and military options make way for other policy options, the U.S. will have a much more difficult time identifying and countering many of the Iran Threat Network's illicit activities, which tend to be irregular or asymmetric in nature. Creating offices of irregular warfare in various government agencies would go a long way toward exposing and damaging the criminal foundations of the Iran Threat Network. While irregular warfare is usually the domain of the military, several operationally robust and aggressive nonkinetic initiatives should be considered. In the area of Information Operations, for example, covert influence authorities ''with teeth'' are necessary to more effectively bolster Iranian moderates in Iran and to undermine Iran's message to audiences in Africa, Central Asia, and across the Middle East. In the still developing area of Counter Threat Finance, the Treasury Department should be put on a financial and economic warfare footing, or better integrated with interagency partners who possess the needed level of financial operational authorities and capabilities. Treasury needs to be more involved in financial operations, particularly overseas, where there are significant gaps of understanding in the areas of international banking and finance. Finally, the U.S. cannot do it alone. The Iran Threat Network has grown increasingly transnational, making it critical to have the support of foreign liaison partners who have the ability to hit Iran's threat facilitation networks (transport, shipping agents, freight forwarders, warehouses, pilots, airlines, etc.). Properly incentivizing our partners to conduct higher impact operations against the Iran Threat Network depends on creativity, money, and persistence. The Rewards for Justice Program, or a version thereof, should offer payouts to exceptional foreign government officials or units who successfully assist U.S. Government initiatives.

CONCLUSION

A nuclear deal with Iran will bring in hundreds of billions of dollars as Iran recoups frozen assets, exports more oil, takes in foreign direct investment, enters into trade agreements, and starts to shrug off its pariah status. Yet, the strategic calculus of the Supreme Leader and much of the ruling conservative establishment is the same today as it was when the Islamic Revolution began: preserving the regime at home and deterring threats from abroad, while externalizing the revolution and resistance. The Iran Threat Network, free of budgetary constraints and emboldened as a newly minted nuclear power, is the engine of the regime and will resume Iran's pursuit of broader goals in the region. Look for a return to past levels of activity by elements of the Iran Threat Network, including units of the Quds Force, whose budgets have been cut back as a result of Iran's economic downturn. This means more operations in Syria, where Iran will continue to work closely with the Assad regime and Iran-trained, equipped, and guided militant networks; further attempts to support Shia activism in Bahrain, where Iran has attempted several times to create the conditions for regime change; continued use of Iraq as a transit point for illicit commerce coming from the gulf, and the movement of men, money, and illicit materiel across the Levant; deeper support to Hezbollah and the newly formed Palestinian coalition government; and likely increases in training, weapons, and funding to the Houthi rebels in Yemen and pariah states such as the Sudan.

GCC countries will continue to harbor deep suspicion, distrust, and enmity toward Iran, well aware of Iran's unrelenting efforts to create internal dissent and destabilization through support to local Shia opposition movements. Still, they will refrain from pursuing their own nuclear programs (other than the UAE) and continue to rely instead on strong bilateral security partnerships with the United States. For its part, Iran will push Hezbollah to do some of its more complicated bidding in Arab countries, which Hezbollah sometimes agrees to, other times not. Finally, the peaceful intentions of a nuclear Iran will take decades to validate. Until that happens, expect more denial, deception, and dissimulation from the Iran Threat Network.

The CHAIRMAN. Thank you.
Dr. Kagan.

STATEMENT OF DR. FREDERICK W. KAGAN, CHRISTOPHER DeMUTH CHAIR AND DIRECTOR, CRITICAL THREATS PROJECT, AMERICAN ENTERPRISE INSTITUTE, WASHINGTON, DC

Dr. KAGAN. Thank you, Chairman Menendez, Ranking Member Corker, I have rarely felt more superfluous as a witness since I agree with virtually everything that the two previous witnesses have said. I will do my best to try to add a little bit to that, but I am afraid this is not going to be a very confrontational hearing, at least in terms of the witnesses.

As I wrote this testimony, I was watching Iraq die. I was reading the reports of the fall of Mosul to the Islamic State of Iraq and al-Sham, to the collapse of the Iraqi Security Forces in the north, to the really complete collapse of the Iraqi Security Forces not only in Ninewah province but also in Kirkuk and wondering whether and where they may be able to stop the ISIS advance, which is not at all clear at this point.

I note that ISIS has been simultaneously conducting operations against its rival al-Qaeda affiliate, Jabhat al-Nusra, in Syria where it continues to expand and to control large amounts of territory. Sectarian conflict in the region is continuing to expand and deepen, along with al-Qaeda safe havens and capabilities.

You might ask what does this have to do with the topic of today's hearing, and I would say that this has everything to do with the topic of today's hearing. Iran is a belligerent in this regional sectarian war, and its regional activities will be shaped to a considerable degree by the approach it adopts in this conflict. We can only reflect on the implications of a possible nuclear weapons deal for the region in the context of how the Iranians are going about, and will go about, pursuing what they perceive to be their interests in the region.

The nuclear issue is at the core of America's thinking about Iran with the exception of this committee, for which I am very grateful. But it is at the periphery of Iran's strategic calculus in many ways. The purpose of pursuing a nuclear weapons program for Iran is to enable other activities in the region. And so from the standpoint of what the Iranians will do in the region, with or without a deal, we have to understand that the nuclear program was never the central objective. It was a means to an end.

I think the point that Ambassador Ross made about whether a deal would constitute a fundamental change in the attitudes of Iran toward the United States and the West is an important one. I think we should reflect on the atmosphere of United States-Soviet relationships during and after the SALT talks. We had a brief period of detente during which the Soviets stopped none of the activities that they had been engaged in against the United States and its allies and around the world, and indeed, the period of detente ended with the Soviet invasion of Afghanistan.

There is no reason—in fact, there is ample reason from the history of arms control agreements to believe that arms control agreements do not generally lead to peace and brotherhood and kumbaya moments. They can occur in the midst of extremely tense engagements as one side or both sides decide that it is not in their interest to pursue a particular weapons path at this time and prefer to take that problem off the table.

But even if we could imagine a total change in the attitudes of the Islamic Republic toward us, which in my opinion would require the death of Ayatollah Khamenei who is absolutely never going to change his views on us, and his replacement by someone who has fundamentally different views, we would still have a problem. That would not actually bring Iran into alignment with our interests in the region. And I think we really have to understand this point.

I began this testimony talking about Iraq because Iran's strategy in Iraq and Syria and Lebanon and Bahrain and Yemen and throughout the region has shown the enormous damage the Islamic Republic does by the methods that it uses to pursue its aims. Iran does not fill vacuums. Iran creates vacuums on the whole. Iran does not strengthen regional states. Iran undermines regional states because its preferred methods are through nonstate or sub-state proxies.

And it is interesting—not surprising, but interesting—to see the way as Lebanese Hezbollah has come into the Lebanese Government, it has, nevertheless, remained an independent force that the Lebanese Government does not control, and the Iranians have assisted it to do so. And in fact, it has engaged in a unilateral invasion of Syria at Iranian behest, which the Lebanese Government certainly did not approve of.

We have seen this in Iraq as well. Iranian efforts in Iraq have consistently undermined efforts to form coherent governance in Iraq even when you have had an Iraqi Shia Prime Minister, although I have never been in the camp of thinking that Malaki was an Iranian stooge.

They are pursuing a similar approach in Yemen. They have co-opted to a considerable extent the quasi-Shia al-Houthis movement in northwest Yemen. And some years ago, we began to see for the first time al-Houthis running around chanting ''death to America'' and repeating Iranian slogans. And the al-Houthis have now established a de facto state independent of the government of Sana'a and are, in fact, working to extend that state. But the Iranians did not support only the al-Houthis. They are also supporting the Southern Mobility Movement, the secessionist movement that is a Sunni movement in southern Yemen. In other words, the Iranian strategy in Yemen, which is, I would submit, in some respects more well thought through than ours, is a strategy that is fundamentally aimed at dismembering the Yemeni state.

All of this would seem odd because we imagine the Iranians to be the enemies of al-Qaeda and threatened by al-Qaeda. And they certainly are threatened by al-Qaeda. But it is interesting that Iranian operatives in Syria have made no effort that we can see to go after the Islamic State of Iraq and al-Sham. And on the contrary, Assad's forces have been largely cooperating with ISIS because ISIS has been taking the fight to the Kurds and the Assad regime finds that of utility.

So the point is that it is not simply that the Iranians do not like us. It is not simply that they are opposed to our interests. We can discuss whether the regime is evil or not, whether it matters or not, whether it is evil. What matters is that this regime is entirely committed to a set of strategies that revolve around a certain set of tools and approaches that are absolutely destabilizing to the region and absolutely fueling the sectarian regional war that is actually the most important American national security threat that we are facing because that regional sectarian war not only destroys any prospect of stability in a critically important region, but it is also the principal recruiting force for a global jihadi movement that is now regularly drawing recruits from the United States itself into these conflicts and most likely cycling them back.

So anything that we do with Iran, deal or no deal, we must develop a strategy, as Ambassador Ross suggested, to compete with the Iranian means and methods and approaches in the Middle East because we must be prepared to contest with Iran not for control of the Middle East, not for Middle East hegemony, not for ideology, but for stability. It is very important to us that we have a peaceful and stable Middle East, and because the word ''stability'' is misused here very frequently, let me say I do not believe that stability flows from the gun of a dictator. I believe that we actually have to have some kind of representative state, some kind of inclusive government, some kind of support from the population. But that is not what the Iranians seek. So if we have any prospect of achieving our core national security objectives in the region, whether we have a nuclear deal or not, we must develop and execute a comprehensive strategy to press our interests in stability and contest the Iranian drive for instability in the region.

Thank you.

[The prepared statement of Dr. Kagan follows:]

PREPARED STATEMENT OF DR. FREDERICK W. KAGAN

Chairman Menendez, Ranking Member Corker, members of the committee, thank you for this opportunity to appear before you today. As I write this testimony, I am reading reports of the fall of Mosul to the Islamic State of Iraq and al-Sham (ISIS) and the military maneuver of ISIS forces toward Baghdad. The Iraqi Security Forces in Ninewah have collapsed, and it is not clear where— or if—they will be able to stop the ISIS advance. ISIS is simultaneously conducting offensive operations against the rival al-Qaeda affiliate in eastern Syria, where it continues to control and govern significant territory. Sectarian conflict in the region continues to expand and deepen, along with al-Qaeda safe havens and capabilities.

What does this have to do with the topic of today's hearing, you might be wondering. The answer is: everything. Iran is a belligerent in this regional sectarian war and its regional activities will be shaped to a considerable degree by the approach it adopts to this conflict. We can only reflect on the implications of a possible nuclear weapons deal for the region in this context.

The national security policy of the Islamic Republic of Iran is designed to prevail in the war Tehran believes the United States and Israel are waging against it. Supreme Leader Khamenei declared in March that international sanctions on Iran became ''an all-out war'' against Iran in 2011. He denied that sanctions have anything to do with Iran's nuclear program: ''One day, their excuse is the nuclear issue and another day, it is the issue of the enrichment. One day, it is human rights and another day, it is other such issues. Sanctions existed against us before the nuclear issue was brought up and they will continue to exist . . . even if the nuclear issue and these negotiations are resolved.'' He sees American enmity in everything: ''From the beginning the enemy has made extensive efforts, and the more we advance, the clearer their work becomes. They use thousands of TV networks, radio programs, and the Internet to curse the Islamic Republic.'' He even blames us for al-Qaeda: ''Today Takfiri groups are working against Islam and Shias in certain regions and carrying out evil acts, but they are not the main enemies. The main enemy is the one who provokes them and provides them with money.'' Even the supposedly reformist Ayatollah Hashemi Rafsanjani declared in 2010: ''Radical Islamic groups such as al-Qaeda and the Taliban are the creatures of the espionage service of the United States and the West.''

These are not isolated statements. The Iranian national security leadership regularly repeats and expands on them. Tehran has evolved a national security strategy around the concept of "soft war" that seeks to defeat the supposedly subtle and complex efforts of the U.S. and Israel to destroy Iran with everything from smart missiles to Internet pornography. This strategy sees any American influence in the Middle East as anathema and a mortal threat, and its goal is the complete expulsion of the U.S., the destruction of Israel, and the creation of a Persian hegemony. The Islamic Republic sees itself as the revolutionary vanguard that will overturn the current immoral, unjust, and infidel world-order in favor of its preferred religious-ideological vision.

Iran seeks to be not merely a great-power rival to the U.S., but a force to destroy the U.S.-dominated (from Tehran's perspective) world system.

The nuclear issue is at the core of America's current policy concern with Iran, but it is at the periphery of Iran's strategic calculus. The rational explanation for Iran's pursuit of nuclear weapons capability is the desire to be able to deter an American or Israeli attack on Iran once and for all. That is a defensive objective whose primary aim is to enable other operations to achieve Iran's goals throughout the region. Iran's nuclear program is meant to be a strategic enabler, not a strategy unto itself.

What would happen, then, if Iran actually abandoned that program? The international sanctions regime would be unwound, large amounts of money and human capital would flow into Iran, the regime would be able to stabilize itself internally and would have enormously greater resources with which to pursue its regional goals. A nuclear agreement would advance the regional interests of the U.S. only if it led to a fundamental change in the nature of Iran's attitudes toward and relationship with the U.S. and its allies.

Such a shift seems most unlikely, however. The entire ideological foundation of the current Iranian regime rests as much on anti-Americanism as it does on anti-Zionism (without much distinction between the two). One could imagine a nuclear deal in which Iran yields almost all of its enrichment capability in exchange for full sanctions relief, but the tone of the agreement would be like the tone of U.S.-Russian relations after the signing of the SALT treaty in 1972. There might well follow a period of detente, but there is no reason to imagine a wholesale change in the fundamental thinking, strategy, and approach of the Islamic Republic. The history of arms treaties amply demonstrates the degree to which the spirit of cooperation in which they are negotiated can be separated from an overall atmosphere of hostility.

But even a total reversal of Tehran's attitudes toward the U.S. would not be enough to bring Iran into alignment with U.S. interests in the region. I began this testimony speaking about Iraq because Iran's strategy there and in Syria, Lebanon, Bahrain, Yemen, and throughout the region has shown the enormous damage the Islamic Republic does to regional stability through the methods by which it pursues its aims. Iran relies mainly on substate Shia militant groups combined with overt bribes to individuals and regimes to shape the strategies and policies of its neighbors.

Lebanese Hezbollah, its primary regional proxy, participates in the Lebanese Government but maintains its own large armed force—which it sent into Syria at Tehran's behest in support of Assad. Iranian strategy in Lebanon has consistently sought to prevent the Lebanese Government from gaining control over Hezbollah—and thereby over much of southern Lebanon—even after Hezbollah became part of the government.

Iranian strategy in Iraq has turned heavily on supporting and sustaining multiple competing Shia militia groups, political factions, and suborned individuals. This strategy has consistently hindered efforts to form a coherent Iraqi state. The militias themselves became a major driver of sectarian conflict from shortly after the U.S. invasion, in fact, and are responsible in no small way for the regional sectarian war we now face.

Tehran has pursued a similar approach in Yemen, coopting the quasi-Shia al-Houthis in the northwest, training, arming, and funding them as they have established a de facto independent ministate between Yemen and Saudi Arabia. Iran simultaneously has been providing assistance to Sunni separatists in southern Yemen, contributing to the collapse of that state.

And Iranian strategy in Syria has been to back Assad in the conduct of a sectarian bloodletting of remarkable viciousness. That viciousness has powerfully fueled the regional sectarian war and become a magnet, rallying cry, and now training and logistical base for Sunni extremists from around the world.

It is not just that the Islamic Republic is anti-American. The Islamic Republic is a polarizing sectarian force whose main methods of pursuing its goals destroy order, stability, and politics. It will seek to manage the escalating crisis through these methods and will instead make it worse. A nuclear deal will only give Tehran more resources with which to pursue its mistaken and misshapen strategy.

A nuclear agreement that verifiably eliminated Iran's ability to acquire nuclear weapons capability would of course be desirable, although I do not believe that it is achievable. Certainly Tehran has not put anything on the table thus far that comes even close to meeting this standard. The Iranian penchant for pursuing secret nuclear and weaponization programs and admitting to them only after the U.S. finds them does not bode well for full transparency, particularly considering the Iranian conviction that the International Atomic Energy Agency is an espionage network for the West. There is also the question of how to ensure continued Iranian adherence to any agreement in the absence of sanctions. Sanctions have been absolutely essential in bringing the Supreme Leader to the negotiating table at all. Once lifted, they will not be easily or quickly restored. Without the credible threat of the rapid restoration of crippling sanctions, pressure on Tehran to abide by any agreement will be considerably less than the pressure that has been required to bring Iran to the table. Even a deal could only work, then, if the Iranians really undergo a fundamental change of heart on the nuclear issue—something for which there is no evidence whatever to suggest.

Any deal comes with the risk of miscalculation and betrayal—the risk that Iran might after all retain the ability to field a nuclear arsenal. We are all focused on that risk. But a deal would also come with another risk—the risk that the U.S. would persuade itself that solving one problem solves all. In this case, on the contrary, solving one problem may very well make others a lot worse. But deal or no deal, the U.S. can only hope to advance (or defend) its interests in the Middle East through our own active engagement. Perhaps we must now speak of reengagement after the determined retreats of the past 5 years.

This is not a brief for military regime change in Iran, for reinvading Iraq, or for any specific policy. It is certainly not an argument for pursuing purely military responses to regional problems and the Iranian threat. We must instead use the moment of reflection afforded by this hearing to consider how to develop a strategy that competes with Iran while fighting al-Qaeda—all the while avoiding the trap of imagining that the one can be an effective ally against the other.

The basic outlines of such a strategy are clear. The urgency of the situations in Iraq and Syria demands active American involvement in those conflicts, not necessarily through the deployment of U.S. combat troops, but certainly through the deployment of advisers, support elements, enablers (including air power), and intelligence to assist the majorities in both countries who seek to reject both al-Qaeda and Iranian domination. Hezbollah's invasion of Syria has exacerbated rifts within Lebanon and opened the possibility of driving a wedge between Hezbollah and other parts of Lebanese society. Aggressive diplomacy and well-targeted assistance could help weaken Hezbollah's control over its vital base, forcing it to refocus on Lebanon and away from supporting Assad. The U.S. must also work seriously—and not through speeches—to regain the confidence of our Arab allies, particularly Saudi Arabia and Turkey. America's retreat from the region has increased the costs of implementing such a strategy, but we must keep in mind that things are not going terribly well for Iran either, despite the current euphoria in Tehran. A strategy that combines continued sanctions with meaningful efforts to displace and disrupt Iran's proxies and Iran's strategies in the region is essential to creating any prospect of long-term change in Tehran's attitudes and of regional stability.

I thank the committee for raising this important issue and for the opportunity to present my views.

The CHAIRMAN. Thank you all.

A lot to cover here. Let me say I see the GCC and others increasingly warming up to Iran. Last month, Saudi Arabia extended an invitation to Foreign Minister Zarif. Last week, the Emir of Kuwait made an official visit to Iran. It seems that President Rouhani may have been invited to the Egyptian President's inauguration ceremony. These are just a few examples, but it seems that Iran's international and regional isolation may be quickly melting away as the anticipation of a deal accelerates.

What is motivating the culf leaders to engage Iran, especially after listening to your description, Ambassador Ross, about their concerns, which while the nuclear deal is something that is really a concern about their regional designs, in terms of engaging the Iranians? Is this hedging? And if so, what does that stem from?

Ambassador Ross. First, I think we probably have to distinguish between some of the different actors in the region on the Arab side.

The Saudi willingness to at least invite Zarif to come—by the way, he has not come yet. I would read that through a very careful lens. They may be prepared to talk to him, but I do not see any sign that the Saudis are about to somehow change their behavior toward the Iranians. Having a conversation with Zarif might be designed to sort of, A, impose a set of principles that if the Iranians want to see any improvement with the Saudis, this is what the Saudis require. And there is a lot of indication that is kind of what the message has been. Or, B, it could just be to see if there is any information they can acquire out of this kind of an exchange. But I do not see the Saudis at this point, certainly not with this King who is very clear on his view of the Iranians—I do not see a change there.

In the case of Kuwait, historically the Kuwaitis had a different kind of relationship with the Iranians. They tried to be somewhat more in between, and they view the Iranians as a potential threat. They lined up more with the Saudis and the Emiratis in terms of their attitudes in the past year when they uncovered what was a plot within Kuwait. But I suspect right now the more traditional instinct to at least hedge bets or at least try to minimize—give the Iranians a reason to reduce reasons for hostility—I think that probably accounts for it.

In the case of Egypt, look, Egypt's focus is much more internal than anything else. They are not going to do anything with Iran that would upset the Saudis. The Saudis are their principal bankers right now. That is their main focus. I think inviting the Iranians to the inauguration is more a sign of trying to demonstrate a broad participation with regard to that event.

If you are talking about Oman, Oman has always had a different relationship with Iran.

Qatar also has always tried to hedge its bets.

The Chairman. You do not see a hedging of bets?

Ambassador Ross. Not right now, not by the Saudis.

The Chairman. So in this context, there are voices that I consistently hear, some in the Congress, others from beyond the Congress, who suggest that striking the nuclear deal with Iran is opening the doors to a much wider set of possibilities. As I listened to your collective testimony, it seems to me it does not open the door to a much wider set of possibilities of engaging Iran in a way in which they will change, particularly the asymmetric effort that they have within the region and beyond but will actually fuel the possibility for them to pursue a course of action that they already determined is in their interest. Is that a fair statement?

Ambassador Ross. Certainly the way I read it. What I was trying to get at was it may well be that Rouhani and Zarif represent a constituency within Iran that would like to end Iran's isolation, would like to normalize relations, see that the best way to support the future of the Islamic Republic is, in fact, to have a greater normalization. Now, obviously, the Supreme Leader I think operates on a different premise. Somehow he was persuaded to give Rouhani a license to negotiate because the costs of isolation, the costs of the sanctions was seen as potentially threatening the Islamic Republic itself.

But for him, he views us through a lens of hostility. He allows the IRGC al-Quds Forces to be their action arm throughout the rest of the region. There is no indication that Rouhani or Zarif have any impact on what the Iranians are doing throughout the rest of the region. And that was what I was trying to suggest. If you want to try to see a constituency that seems more pragmatic to have greater authority and somehow greater empowerment, the way to do that is to show the high costs of the behaviors that are unacceptable throughout the rest of the region.

And I would also say, also the only way he is going to be able to sell the Supreme Leader on the kind of deal that is required, by the way, outlines of which I completely agree with what you presented—that is what is required for us to have a deal. The reason I say I do not think a deal is likely—Scott thinks a deal may happen. Here I would say I am more dubious. I am not saying it will not happen, but it is not going to happen unless there is an understanding that they get no relief on sanctions. They get no economic benefit unless, in fact, they roll back their program. Their approach to the negotiations right now is we will do some semblance of transparency and we should be able to add to the rest of the program. I do not believe there will be a deal under those circumstances.

The CHAIRMAN. Let me ask you all this, and I would like to have your opinion. Former CIA Director General David Petraeus said in an op-ed published in the Washington Post—and I quote—"rather than freeing Washington to reduce the U.S. footprint in the Middle East and focus elsewhere, a nuclear agreement with Tehran is likely to compel us to deepen our military, diplomatic, and intelligence presence in the region in order to help partners there balance against increasing Iranian power. A variety of steps should be pursued to this end: approval of additional military capability sought by Arab partners and Israel, a renewed initiative to integrate the Gulf Cooperation Council countries' air and ballistic missile defenses, maritime and air exercises to demonstrate U.S. and partner capabilities in the region, and sustaining, if not augmenting, existing infrastructure and force posture there."

That is a pretty significant universe of things. How do you all feel about that? Dr. Kagan, let us start with you.

Dr. KAGAN. I am in violent agreement with that. A nuclear deal that lifts sanctions to any considerable extent will result in a flood of money resources, intellectual property, human capital, and other things into Iran. There are companies and countries around the world champing at the bit to get into a potentially massive and extremely lucrative market. That will flood the coffers of the state. We know that it will also flood the coffers of the IRGC.

It has been interesting to observe the behavior of the IRGC leaders and their statements as these negotiations have proceeded. Initially they were very cold, very cautious, very suspicious, and very hostile. Now they are very supportive. They are constantly underlining their support for Rouhani and for what he is doing, and they are very clearly on board. And it is the behavior more of people

23

who believe that they are really going to get something out of this than people who have been simply told by the Supreme Leader to get in line.

So I think the assessment that the Iranian threat in the region will grow enormously is absolutely spot-on because I think Ambassador Ross has really hit it. I am not as sure that in strengthening Rouhani per se is going to achieve our interests. I am very confident that until and unless the strategy that Qasem Soleimani has been pursuing is shown to be bad for Iran and bad for the Supreme Leader in some way, the Iranians will continue to double down on that strategy.

The CHAIRMAN. Mr. Modell, do you have any views?

Mr. MODELL. I would tend to agree. I think that with the influx of cash that comes as a result of a deal—and first of all, I would like to clarify that. I think the world will be presented with a deal. I do not know how good the deal is going to be because every indication I have is that Iran does not have any true intentions of actually honoring its obligation—that has been very clear since the November agreement—to actually come clean on the military dimensions of its program which, as far as we know, in the latest IAEA Board of Governors report, at the present time they are not actually implementing the additional protocol and they have not answered a lot of the fundamental questions about the military dimensions of the program, the most troubling aspects of the program. So whatever that deal is, we have a very, very long way to go before we can actually call it a comprehensive deal.

But to the extent that Petraeus pointed out that there is going to be an enhanced focus on the Middle East, I could not agree more because the necessity of coming up with a comprehensive verification and compliance regime is going to demand even greater focus on all of the things that Iran does to evade sanctions. And a lot of those mechanisms are in the region. A lot of the ways in which they would potentially cheat on any type of a nuclear deal, which I believe is very likely—they basically obligate us to actually sort of double up our resources in figuring out what they are doing.

As far as going back to the GCC issue, I want to make one comment. I very much agree. I think behind the charm offensive, I think when you talk to the Saudis and you talk to the Kuwaitis and others, I think they see through it. I think there is too much scar tissue over the last 30 years for them to simply embrace Iran. I think the existence of Hezbollah of the Hejaz years ago, which was used by Iran to attack targets in Saudi, other Hezbollah entities that were backed by Iran that are well known in the gulf left them with a very permanent, lasting impression that Iran has broader regional roles that are contrary to their own. And they are going to continue to focus on their internal security, and they will keep Iran at bay, to the extent they can. So I agree with the idea that there is going to have to be a greater focus on the Middle East, and there is going to be no pivot away from it.

Ambassador ROSS. I support what Petraeus was suggesting. The only difference I would have is I would not wait until after the deal. I would do it now. I would try to do each of those things now. And I think, again, it makes a deal more likely.

The CHAIRMAN. Senator Corker.

Senator CORKER. Thank you, Mr. Chairman.

And I do want to say to the witnesses a great compliment as the chairman let each of you go over about 3 minutes in your testimony. And that just speaks to the importance we place on each of you. So thank you so much for being here.

Mr. Ross, I know you have read the quote recently from the Supreme Leader of Iran saying today launching a military attack is not a priority from the viewpoint of Americans. They understand that they suffered a loss on the issue of Iraq and Afghanistan where they launched military attacks. There it can be said that they have changed their mind about launching a military attack.

I am just curious as to how important that statement, that thinking process is relative to the negotiations that are underway.

Ambassador ROSS. I think it is fundamental. I think the Supreme Leader has got to believe that the price of the failure of diplomacy is simply unacceptable from his standpoint, and I think the extent to which he believes that when we say all options are on the table, he believes that they are not—that is what his statement means—I think it makes the prospect of diplomacy succeeding less than it would be otherwise.

Senator CORKER. And does anybody dissent?

Dr. KAGAN. No. I would go even further than that and say that what we are seeing, as we observe the statements of the Iranian military command, is a sense of triumphalism in Tehran that is remarkable. They really do appear to believe that they have defeated us in a very fundamental way, and that the nuclear deal will cement that defeat. So very far from feeling as if they are in a position of weakness and must concede things. I think the talks are most likely to fail in many respects because the Iranians think that they do not have to give us anything because they think they have already won.

Senator CORKER. While you have got the mike, your comment about the strategy that Iran is displaying in the region of dismembering, of destabilizing—one of the things I did not pick up in that discussion was toward what end. In other words, the role they are playing is very evident, but from their perspective, that is toward what end in the region?

Dr. KAGAN. It is toward the larger objective of Iranian regional hegemony and the establishment of a Shia crescent and the overthrow of states and peoples that they think have been unjustly ruling in areas of concern to themselves and to the establishment of solid proxies for themselves. And since they have not historically been able to make states proxies for a variety of reasons, they have become accustomed to working through certain kinds of proxies, in addition to which I would say that I think although the Iranians have a general destination in mind, a general vision of what they would like the region to look like, I am not persuaded that they have a very specific vision. And I am not persuaded that they are driving toward very particular end states in any of the countries that they are actually supporting. They are driving in a direction, and the direction is greater Iranian influence, driving the United States out of the region, isolating Israel, and empowering people who will pursue the ideology of the Islamic Republic and, more importantly, the interests of the Islamic Republic.

Senator CORKER. So, therefore, controlling the region but not necessarily through statehood but just through proxies and gaining strength in that way.

Dr. KAGAN. I think, obviously, they preferred the situation when Assad was governing Syria. The situation that they now have in Syria is much worse for them than it was before. But it does not seem to be that much of a priority for them, honestly, to build up the capacity of states as long as they can maintain the effective capacity of nonstate proxies.

Senator CORKER. Does anybody disagree with that thesis?

[No response.]

Mr. MODELL. If you would not mind, I would like to make a comment just on the mind-set of the Supreme Leader very quickly.

One of the things that has been mentioned here is that there is doubt as to whether or not the Supreme Leader thinks that any nuclear deal, good or bad, is going to lead to a greater rapprochement with the United States and the West. Based on everything that I have been reading lately on the Iranian side in the Iranian press, including the comments that were just mentioned, I think one of his redlines, if you had to actually define it, is exactly that. He does not believe that any type of agreement—it may lead to the revival of the Iranian economy, but the resumption of diplomatic relations with the United States at this point is definitely a redline. And I do not think that he would go there.

There has been mention of Soleimani and his influence particularly with the Supreme Leader. When you look at the way that Iran has carried out its foreign policy in the Levant and Iraq, Soleimani has had a great deal of control. And Rouhani came into office knowing that to actually come in and try to take away influence from Soleimani in the area of foreign policy in the immediate region—I think he realized that was unrealistic. And I think to date you are seeing Soleimani still really calling the shots when it comes to what Iran does and what Iran is planning to do in that part of the world. And I do not think you are going to see a change on that.

Ambassador ROSS. I will just comment briefly on what Dr. Kagan said. I generally agree with him. When the Supreme Leader now takes a look at what is happening in Iraq, that is not a good thing. Their preoccupation with Iraq is something that is understandable. They fought a war for 8½ years. And with ISIS establishing itself and moving toward Baghdad, this is a challenge. This is a threat. So dismembering of states is a lever they have. It is a tool they have. I agree with what you said, that having someone like Assad in control of Syria where you are not consuming lots of resources, where you are not having to expend a lot of these proxies that you develop, they were using Hezbollah, Qutb Hezbollah, within Syria. Now they are going to have to mobilize all these Shia groups again and militias back in Iraq. So that is not a great scenario for them.

Senator CORKER. So let me flip it around. So you have laid out what you think Iran's thesis is, what their strategy is, what their objective is. If you look at U.S. policy, what is its objective? I mean, if you look at what happened in Syria, we basically have purposely strengthened Assad by focusing on chemical weapons. I have said this many times. The wisest thing he did for his own sustainability was to kill 1,200 people with chemical weapons, and that is all the administration now talks about is that. And yet, he has just been reelected, quote, quote, quote, to another term.

In Iraq, you see what is happening. There is a guy named George Friedman who wrote a book that was the rage for a while talking about the next decade and how the United States really should cozy up with Iran. Is that really where we should be? I mean, if you look at the administration's policies—I mean, one, two, three, four—it would seem that that is the direction they are taking.

Do you think that is something that is purposeful? Do you think this is by accident? What is the United States policy today relative to Iran?

Ambassador ROSS. Well, the way I would read the administration's policy is to focus on the nuclear issue first, to prevent the Iranians from being in a position where having civil nuclear power can be converted into a nuclear weapon. I think that is a genuine objective. I think that is what the administration is pursuing through negotiations.

I think it is prepared to work with our friends in the region to counter what the Iranians are doing throughout the rest of the region. Obviously, at this point, the way the regional actors see it is that they do not have a high level of confidence that we are prepared to be active enough to counter the Iranians because they believe that our priority of the nuclear objective is so great that everything else is secondary. That is one of the reasons I said I would like to see us—some of the things I even suggested that we should be doing in the aftermath of an agreement I am actually suggesting we should be doing now because, A, it sends a message to our friends we are not prepared to sit back and acquiesce in seeing the landscape and the region change fundamentally against the interests of our friends shifting in favor of the Iranians. I think that would do wonders for our friends. But I think, as I said before, it would actually do wonders to actually reach an agreement.

I do think the Supreme Leader makes a calculus about whether something is a threat to the well-being of the Islamic Republic. I do not think it is an accident that Rouhani was allowed to win the election. I use the words ''allowed to win the election'' quite deliberately. The Supreme Leader decided that the costs were too high of staying on the path they were on. So if you want to reach an agreement, it has to be clear that the costs are very high if you do not reach an agreement. And I think the more the administration can communicate that, they will do better not only in terms of their objective on the nuclear issue, but they will do better on their objective in the rest of the region as well.

Senator CORKER. If you could briefly respond, Dr. Kagan, I would appreciate it. I know my time is way up.

Dr. KAGAN. Senator, what I would say is that what the administration is actually doing in the region has had the effect generally of putting us on the side of Iran in the region rather than on the side of other potential partners. I have no idea whether that is deliberate, and I am reluctant to think that it is. I think it is a corollary of policies that are really focused on not being involved in the region and on seeing al-Qaeda as the principal threat in the region, which it is, and on seeing Iranian proxies as, in many respects, our best bet for containing the al-Qaeda threat without United States involvement, which I believe is a very bad miscalculation.

Senator CORKER. Thank you.

The CHAIRMAN. Thank you.

Senator Cardin.

Senator CARDIN. Thank you, Mr. Chairman.

I do thank all three of our witnesses. I have found this discussion to be very, very helpful.

Obviously, the best outcome would be for an agreement to be reached that accomplishes what the chairman spelled out—an agreement that eliminates a breakout capacity for Iran in a short period of time and that ensures it will not be a nuclear weapons state. Listening to your testimonies, none of the three of you believe that that is likely to occur within the timeframe set out for this agreement.

And it seems to me that the United States can influence one of two outcomes at the end of July. One could be that we have not achieved the objective of preventing Iran from breaking out to a nuclear capacity, and we certainly do not have the transparency that was needed. And therefore, we should work with our international partners to continue and to expand the sanctions that are imposed against Iran because of their violations of their international commitments. We must try to keep those sanctions as strong as possible, looking for a new day and a new opportunity to advance our objectives of preventing Iran from becoming a nuclear weapons state.

Or the second option could be, well, we have a framework. Let us build on it. Let us make sure that we have transparency to prevent Iran from continuing its nuclear program. Let us try to make incremental progress in getting them to weaken their capacity as a nuclear weapons state, and let us try to keep the sanctions as tight as we can during that period of time, recognizing there may be some concessions that have to be made as progress is made.

It seems to me they are the two paths that we could go down. And it does seem to me that the United States is the driver as to which of those two courses we take since we are the dominant player in these negotiations.

I think I know your answers, but I would like to get on the record what you think is in the best interest of the United States. Which of those two courses would be in our best interest?

Dr. KAGAN. Well, let us go from junior to senior.

I think what Ambassador Ross has outlined is the right course of action, which is we should yield as little as possible in advance of the continuation of the negotiations and throughout the negotiations. We need to make it very clear that there is an enormous amount of pain for Iran if it does not come through with an agreement of the sort that is required and we all agree on what that is here.

Senator CARDIN. I hear you. I understand that, and I agree with that.

My point is we are going to reach a point where we will either do, as Mr. Modell suggested, announce that there is some interim agreement—it will not be a complete agreement, as Mr. Modell is expressing. But the United States could influence a judgment to say that is not adequate and therefore we should go back to where we were prior to the beginning of this year and get the international coalition, again recognizing that Iran is not serious about it.

What course do you think is in the best interest for the United States? To continue along the path of holding Iran—I think we are able to do this—to not advancing with transparency and negotiating the process. But the cost of that would be to give in on some of the sanctions. Or are we better off saying no, this is not working?

Dr. KAGAN. Okay. Senator, I will give you the direct answer to that. I apologize. Anyone who has purchased a rug in a Middle Eastern or, as I have, in an Afghan market knows that you have to be prepared to walk away from the table. You have to be prepared to walk out of the shop if the deal is not going toward what you need it to go to. And the worst thing that we can do is make it clear to the Iranians that we want a deal so badly that we will continue to dole out concessions, even as they are not meeting our terms, in the hopes that they will ultimately come to where we want them to be. So I would say at a certain point, if it is clear that they are not going to get there now, we should walk away, and walking away means bringing back as harsh a sanctions regime as we can.

Mr. MODELL. Senator, I would tend to agree. I think even though we are going to be presented with some sort of a deal that is going to take years to verify and confirm if it is real, I would say in the runup to that, we ought to give very serious consideration about making sure that—I agree with what Fred says. We should be willing to say no because I think there are simply too many indications——

Senator CARDIN. Do you disagree with me that the United States is sort of in the driver's seat here from the point of view of whether we are presented with some sort of a deal or saying we have not made enough progress, we are back in square one?

Mr. MODELL. The perception on the Iranian side is that we are not in the driver's seat. If you take at face value everything that they Iranian leaders are saying—and we are talking about the conservative hardliners—they are saying that the Obama administration is more desperate for a deal than Iran is. So I think that they are hoping for an easing of sanctions, and I think they are looking to enter into, quite frankly, a 10- or 20-year process that will allow them to replenish their funds and get the Iran threat network back and get their economy going. And if they do truly have intentions of cheating, they will have plenty of time to do it. So, again, I think there are simply too many unresolved concerns for us to go forward.

Senator CARDIN. I certainly have questions. I am going to give Ambassador Ross a chance.

I think the administration has been clear, though, what an agreement must look like. We have had several discussions about that. So I am not sure I want to identify myself with your view that the administration has already made that judgment. I am not sure they have. And I think that the United States can direct what path we take at the end of July.

Mr. MODELL. No, I agree. I just think there is a difference in perceptions right now.

Senator CARDIN. That is an important point.

Mr. MODELL. There is wishful thinking on the Iranian side that they can actually get to a point where they will have a little bit more flexibility.

Senator CARDIN. Ambassador Ross.

Ambassador ROSS. I do agree with that. I think the Iranians right now think they can get what they want without having to do what is necessary, and I think they are dead wrong. They will not. I do not think the administration is prepared to accept anything. I do think we are not going to get a deal by July 20.

The real question you are asking is do we say, all right, stop it now and go back to the way it was prior to the joint plan of action or do we do what is built already into the joint plan of action, which is by mutual agreement, you can extend it another 6 months. It is clear that the other members of the 5+1 will say let us extend it for the remaining 6 months. I think it will be difficult for the administration under those circumstances to say we are going to cut it off and walk away when the other members want to proceed and when our greatest effectiveness, at least with the sanctions, is when everyone is prepared to continue to implement those sanctions.

Having said that, it is not going to be a given. This will not be a simple negotiation simply to extend because we will say to the Iranians, all right, look. You had to roll back your 20 percent and you have done that. We need to see some other rollback. For example, we need to see some rollback of your 3.5 percent. And the Iranians will say, well, we are not going to do that unless we get something. So it is not a given that you are going to be able to extend this because this itself is going to involve a negotiation.

Right now, our focus is not on that plan B. Our focus is on trying to get a deal by July 20. I just think where the Iranians are is so far from where they need to be, unless this is just purely posturing, unless they are holding out until the last second and suddenly they are going to concede, but I doubt that. That is not the way I think they operate. So I think it is not going to be so simple to produce even the alternative that you are talking about, extending it for another 6 months.

We are going to come to a point if there is no deal by the end of the year, then what do we do. And then I would say we do have to be prepared to walk away. I think we have to show the Iranians we are not so anxious for a deal. The deal we are prepared to accept is one that already involves a major concession to them. The major concession is that they will be allowed to enrich in a limited way. That is a big concession to them. And the price for that has to be that they go along with a very substantial rollback of the numbers of centrifuges, a ship-out of almost all of the enriched uranium material they have in country, a shutdown of Fordow, and Arak being converted into a light water reactor with then answers to the possible military dimensions of their program not because we are seeking to punish them but because how are we going to have a high level of confidence about what is going to happen in the future if they are not prepared to reveal what happened in the past.

Senator CARDIN. Well, I agree with that. And, of course, this morning's report is not very encouraging on those issues. Thank you.

Thank you, Mr. Chairman.

The CHAIRMAN. Let me ask a quick question in response to something you said to Senator Cardin. There is a third option in terms of July 20, and that is you extend but exactly under the same terms and conditions.

Ambassador ROSS. That may be. That could be a fallback in the event. But I think going in, if there is——

The CHAIRMAN. I am not an advocate of that, but I am just saying it is a possibility.

Ambassador ROSS. I think in the end, if you get a rollover, it will be a rollover with them being required to roll something further back and us also easing some additional sanctions.

The CHAIRMAN. Senator Risch.

Senator RISCH. Thank you, Mr. Chairman.

As I listen to what you say, am I correct in getting out of this that all of you think that the administration is not going to wind up with a deal here, that the Iranians are not going to be willing to go far enough that the administration will cut a deal? Briefly. Is that what I am getting out of your testimony?

Ambassador ROSS. By July 20, I think that is right. I am not saying that if we do not find a way to increase the leverage on the Iranians that we could not get a comprehensive deal. But right now, that is not where the Iranians are, and I do not think they think they need to be. And I think they are wrong.

Senator RISCH. Mr. Modell.

Mr. MODELL. I was going to say I think the world is going to be presented with some sort of a deal that is going to have to be worked out over time. I do not know what that deal is going to look like, but the more you look at the Iranians' insistence, just as they did from 2003 to 2005, in having 50,000 centrifuges or 100,000 centrifuges eventually as part of a nationwide civilian nuclear program, I think eventually a deal is bound to come undone.

Senator RISCH. Mr. Kagan.

Dr. KAGAN. Senator, I am not prepared to say what this administration might or might not accept or might or might not announce. So I do not know.

On the Iranian side, I think the likelihood that the Iranians will agree to a deal such as Ambassador Ross has identified and which we all agree is the minimum necessary is zero unless things change very dramatically, and the change is not going to come through diplomacy and negotiations.

Senator RISCH. Well, I guess my fear is that we will wind up with a deal and it is not going to be the deal that needs to be done. I got to tell you after watching negotiations, as this administration has proceeded, I have got a really deep-seated fear in that regard. Anybody want to try to change that for me?

Ambassador ROSS. Yes.

Senator RISCH. Okay, have at it. [Laughter.]

Ambassador ROSS. I believe that the administration understands that on this issue if you produce an outcome that leaves the Iranians in a position where they are a threshold nuclear state, where there are not very clear prohibitions that would make it difficult for them to then turn that into having a nuclear weapons capability, that that is not a sustainable deal. It is not good from the administration's standpoint. It is not good from the national interest standpoint. It is not going to gain support within the Congress. It is certainly not going to get support from key regional friends. And I do not think the administration is negotiating with the Iranians in a way at this point that suggests that they are prepared to cave and not meet a certain basic threshold, which I think in fact is close to what the chairman outlined in his opening statement.

Senator RISCH. Mr. Modell, do you share that optimism?

Mr. MODELL. I do not. I have to disagree on that. I think over the last 4 or 5 years, you have given the Supreme Leader numerous reasons for him to think that the United States will back down, that this President is committed to multilateralism and not confronting the Iranian regime, with the exception of the sanctions regime which we are now actually negotiating right now. But I think there is ample evidence to suggest that we are looking for a deal desperately, and that is what they believe.

Senator RISCH. Mr. Kagan.

Dr. KAGAN. I think the administration is going to be faced at a certain point with a very sharp dilemma as my colleagues on the panel have outlined. I do not feel like I can predict in advance how exactly it will react to that. My concern is that the administration seems to be seeking desperately for some sort of foreign policy success and this is it. And that is a mind-set that can be very dangerous when you are in a negotiation.

Senator RISCH. Thank you.

Mr. Ross, I hope you are right and that Mr. Modell and I are wrong. But in any event, I guess time will tell.

Very quickly. Let us assume we walk out of the rug market. How do we get the genie back in the bottle on the sanctions? We need some partners on this, and I use that word ''partners'' advisedly. One of those partners is Russia. It has been in all the papers. Our relationship has not been the best lately. How do we get the genie back in the bottle?

Ambassador ROSS. Let me just say one thing. When I was asked at the time after the events in Crimea unfolded, was I worried that we would have an immediate problem with the Russians on the Iranian issue, my answer was ''No,'' not immediately because they are not in the 5+1 negotiations as a favor to us. They do not have an interest in the Iranians having a nuclear weapon. So it is not to say if they decided this was the most important thing to us and it trumped everything else and they realized that they could use it as a lever on us on other issues, that they would not do that. They would. But they have their own interests here.

And it is interesting that in the negotiations that have been going on so far—and one of the reasons I think that you have this high-level bilateral discussion that took place this week with the Iranians was precisely because the 5+1 has actually held together in terms of saying that where the Iranians are is not going to make a deal possible.

Now, can I say that will hold forever? I am not so sure. If the Iranians were to suddenly come in and change their position and adopt a position where they offered concessions that fell well short of where we want to be, maybe they would be able to play upon the differences in the 5+1. But that has not been the Iranian behavior so far. And partly—here I agree with my colleagues—it is because the Iranians think they do not have to do it. Well, unless we correct that impression, there is not going to be a deal.

Senator RISCH. I think the thing that has troubled all of us here is we have all watched the media reports about this flood of business people that are going in there and getting ready to do business, as if the sanctions are done and over with. And that really troubles me about trying to put that back in the box. It seems to me it is going to be very difficult.

Mr. Modell, my time is almost up. Do you want to take a run at this real quick?

Mr. MODELL. I was just going to say I agree with Mr. Ross on those comments with regard to the Russian mind-set and the P5+1, but I would also be very careful about disregarding entirely the possibility of a new strategic partnership between Iran and Russia on some level, particularly if we get into a long phased process for 5 or 10 or 20 years where we have to continuously reaffirm that they are following the additional protocol. But it is a tense process. Meanwhile, I think there is a good indication you are going to see growing signs of partnership between Russia and Iran behind the scenes.

Senator RISCH. Thank you.

Mr. Kagan, do you want to close this out for me?

Dr. KAGAN. Yes. I agree what the Russians can do in the P5+1 and so forth may be limited. But I also agree that we are already seeing indications of an Iranian-Russian entente of a much deeper level than we have seen before. And what we have to recognize is that Russia is not a partner anymore. Sadalov Dimeter sees the United States as his enemy and sees himself at war with us. This is extremely clear from his statements and actions. And he sees our enemies as his potential allies. So I think we need to understand that core pillar, that Russian partnership as a core pillar of American strategy toward Iran and Syria—that pillar has collapsed. And we need to contemplate what we are going to do in the aftermath.

Senator RISCH. Thank you.

Thank you, Mr. Chairman.

The CHAIRMAN. Senator Coons.

Senator COONS. Thank you, Chairman Menendez, for chairing this hearing, and I want to thank our witnesses for appearing today as we consider the very difficult potential implications of a nuclear agreement with Iran regionally and globally.

I do share the administration's ultimate goal, stated goal, of reaching an agreement that denies Iran the ability to acquire nuclear weapons capability, and I do continue to hope that a final deal could be reached that would include the most comprehensive inspections and verification regime possible so that we may irrefutably prevent Iran from acquiring a pathway to a bomb.

However, I share the skepticism and concerns expressed by this panel. We should have no illusions about these negotiations. The Iranians have given us no reason to trust their intentions, and any final agreement in my view must dismantle Iran's enrichment infrastructure and address the military dimensions of Iran's nuclear program including particularly its ICBM capability.

So we also have to consider the regional implications and the legitimate and shared security concerns of our vital and trusted allies, principally Israel, and many others in the region.

As the chair of the Africa Subcommittee, I am also increasingly concerned about Iran's not just charm offensive, but active engagement across the continent to find diplomatic and potential military or economic allies as they continue to spread their influence and seek ways to break out from our efforts to impose meaningful sanctions.

Ambassador, as you suggested in your written testimony, there is no deal. There is no pathway to a deal unless the Supreme Leader is convinced that if diplomacy fails, they will be enduring severe economic pain and the high probability that force will be used to destroy the investment that they have made in the nuclear program.

I am cautiously encouraged that the sanctions regime has not come unraveled, that the negotiations have gone this far, and yet sanctions have largely remained effectively in place. And I agree with the dynamics you point to that suggests that the Russians may remain engaged with this at least for the moment.

What do you see as the greatest risk? I agree with Dr. Kagan. Having negotiated in a number of souks around the world, you have to not just be willing to walk away. You have to walk away for there to be a deal.

So what is the most important weak point of our ability to sustain a meaningful, a punishing sanctions regime given that we may well have to walk away?

Ambassador Ross. Well, the weakest point would be if some of the countries that, prior to the joint plan of action, were actually cutting back on their oil purchases stopped doing that. I guess the question is what is the best way to ensure that they do not do that. There are two different mind-sets there.

One is, again, you continue to highlight, look, you do that and you pay this terrible price with us. Now, obviously, that imposes a price on us as well.

The other is to be able to use what is the Iranian nonresponsiveness. Again, when we say walk away, we should be prepared to walk away. But one of the values of having demonstrated a readiness to negotiate genuinely and in good faith is that you expose the Iranians. I said before our readiness to be prepared to allow an outcome where they are allowed to have limited enrichment is a big concession. So if they are allowed to have limited enrichment but they are not prepared to do a deal, one of the things we are doing is we are exposing that. The fact of the matter is they do not want civil nuclear power. They want the option of being able to have a nuclear weapon, and they are not prepared to give it up. Now, the more you can expose that, the more you are going to be able to sustain I think the collective enforcement of sanctions that we have right now.

Senator COONS. Well, Ambassador Ross and Dr. Kagan both, if Iran is allowed to retain some element of a domestic enrichment program, what do you think are the consequences of that? The UAE in a civil nuclear agreement with the United States gave up its enrichment capability, and I think if we get presented with a deal where there is anything other than the most preliminary or basic civil enrichment capability remaining within Iran, I think it has very negative consequences regionally and globally. But I would be interested in what you think.

Ambassador ROSS. Look, there is no question that from a strictly nonproliferation standpoint, the best outcome is no enrichment. But that is probably not something that can be achieved. The question is, what do you say to a country like the UAE? I think what you say to them is look at what is being imposed on them. The kind of verification regime we need is the equivalent of what we had in Iraq. Do you want to have the kind of intrusion? If you want to go ahead with enrichment, that is what is going to be required. You do not have the same kind of sovereignty that you have today. So I would say you can show, yes, you did something that was the right path, but the agreement here that they are adopting is one that imposes limits on them that you would not want to have to face yourself.

Senator COONS. Is it credibly possible for us to sustain an inspection regime over the long term that will actually provide the needed transparency and reassurance to Israel and to the United States?

Ambassador ROSS. Well, it better be. Look, we should not be prepared to agree to an outcome where they have an enrichment capability even if it is limited because we know from their past behavior—you know, the old saying—Ronald Reagan's saying was trust but verify. Well, my approach with the Iranians is distrust and verify. So it better be.

Dr. KAGAN. Senator, if I could take a shot at that, I have got a very direct answer, which is "No." I cannot imagine any verification regime that could actually provide the kind of guarantees that Israel or other allies would require partly because there never has been such an inspection regime.

The Iraq inspection regime, we should remember, failed and it failed in the most interesting possible way. It completely failed to identify the fact that Saddam actually did not have the nuclear program. And as a result, it led everyone in the region to believe that he did, and it led us to believe that he did.

It is hard for me to imagine that it will more effective in a country the size and shape of Iran with the terrain of Iran and with the degree of investment in digging that the Iranians have done.

But I would just like to make one other point very quickly, which is that we are in the process of down-scaling our own intelligence capabilities at a dramatic rate, along with our military footprint and our military capabilities. And you cannot divorce the question of the verifiability of any deal from the question of what our intelligence capabilities are going to be down the road.

Senator COONS. I agree.

Ambassador ROSS. It is a reason, by the way, that you do have to have a very thought-out and preplanned approach to dealing with the consequences of violations.

Senator COONS. If I might ask a last question, Mr. Chairman.

Ambassador, following up on that exact point, there are some publicly expressed concerns by the Israelis about their ability to rely on our security guarantees, and there are some repeatedly expressed concerns by Congress about our level of engagement with oversight for a potential deal and then its execution.

What advice might you have for the administration and for us about reassuring the Israelis and engagement by Congress—by the engagement by the administration with Congress in the advance of our being presented with some deal?

Ambassador ROSS. Well, it is two points that I was making in the testimony. One, we should have a systematic conversation with the Israelis about what cheating could look like, how best to deal with it, and specifically what the actions would be in the event of certain kinds of cheating, including not just sanctions but even the use of force. And we should be prepared to provide the Israelis some additional capabilities, with a clear understanding that if there was cheating and we did not act, we would support their acting and they would have the means to do so.

Senator COONS. Thank you, Ambassador. Thank you to our panel and your testimony.

The CHAIRMAN. Senator Rubio.

Senator RUBIO. Thank you, Mr. Chairman.

Thank you all for being here. Fascinating testimony.

I did not want to miss this opportunity. Today is the fifth anniversary of the fraudulent election that brought Mahmoud Ahmadinejad to power and the protests that followed it. And I highlight this fact because I think that 5 years ago the administration missed an opportunity to stand up for human rights and for the aspirations of the Iranian people in those weeks following that fraudulent election. And I think that has had repercussions since.

In that vein, the general matrix that has been outlined, as we have discussed this issue, has been that these sanctions are in place to deter, punish, and hopefully to encourage Iran to stop enriching and reprocessing because that gives them that basic capability.

And then the second area argument has always been that if in fact they ever break out and go toward a weapon, the word that is always used is all options are on the table. But what that really means is a military option. And yet, I now believe—and I wanted to get your opinion—that more than ever before in recent memory there is a solid opinion now on behalf of the leadership of Iran, especially the Supreme Leader, that the United States is not willing to use military force. I think that he believes that we will use economic sanctions. I think he believes we will use soft power and all sorts of other things, but I do not believe that at any time in recent memory have they believed more strongly than they do now that the United States is not willing and/or capable of using any sort of military force against them potentially no matter what they do. And the implications that that is having on these negotiations I believe are important.

And I wanted to get your sense of whether you believe that that is true, and more importantly, was there ever a time in recent memory where they had perhaps a different opinion or where they perhaps had concerns that the United States, in fact, would engage in some sort of military action? Anyone can go first. If you agree with me, go first, please. [Laughter.]

Mr. MODELL. One of the things I mentioned in my opening comments was exactly that. In 2009, I think the United States missed a major opportunity, probably the first real opportunity in the 30 years at that point to actually effect some sort of a permanent change in the foundation of the regime. We failed to capitalize on that. In 2009, when the movement against the fraudulent elections coalesced into the Green Movement, the people in the Green Movement were wondering what kind of support they should expect from the United States, and that ended up to be no support at all. It was never designed to be a militant move to violently overthrow the regime, but at the same time, it sent a real strong message to the reformist movement in the country that we were not really willing to do anything and that instead, the President was elected on the idea that he was going to engage with anybody, be that Hugo Chavez in Venezuela or the Supreme Leader in Iran, that it was all about engagement. So that started the sort of second track of engagement. But again, it was a very clear message to the Supreme Leader of weakness on his part, and I think that that has been verified over and over and over again.

I think when you look at where we are now, I firmly believe that he thinks that we are here negotiating out of desperation for a deal. And I am not convinced that he thinks we are going to walk away. When he repeatedly makes comments, as the chairman mentioned, that the United States is unwilling to take military action, I think he honestly believes that.

Dr. KAGAN. I think I will pick up the hint that you I think were throwing out there, which is, yes, in 2003 I believe that the Iranian regime and the Supreme Leader thought that Iran could quite possibly be next and really did seriously—much more seriously than the Bush White House—consider the possibility that we would finish in Iraq and pivot to the east and take out the next country in the Axis of Evil.

Senator RUBIO. What did they do as a result of that?

Dr. KAGAN. They suspended the nuclear program and took a variety of steps to conceal it and to try to reach out to us in a variety of ways. More or less, the sincerity of those outreaches is open to question. But, yes, that is clearly what happened.

I would like to parse what you said about their belief in our capability a little bit more finely, though. I do not think the Supreme Leader believes that we do not have the capability to remove him from power if we chose to do so. I think he believes that we do have that capability.

Senator RUBIO. And just to clarify, I did not mean the technical capability. I meant the political capability.

Dr. KAGAN. Exactly.

Senator RUBIO. The political will.

Dr. KAGAN. This is entirely about will.

Ambassador ROSS. I agree that in 2003 they feared that they were next, and they put a proposal on the table. It was just suspension. They actually put a proposal on the table through the Swiss that would have been far-reaching. There was some question was it genuine or not, but it was never really tested.

By 2005, 2006, they had walked away from the suspension without any consequence to them. At a point in 2006, 2007, when we were really tied down in Iraq, they no longer had the same kind of fear.

The Supreme Leader's statement now that we will not use force is something he has not said before. So clearly, they have the perception that we will not. And it is very important for us to change that perception. If we want to have a deal, we have to change that perception.

Senator RUBIO. I would highlight, as you—I think maybe someone mentioned this earlier on the June 4 speech. It was underneath a banner that said America cannot do a damn thing. They have used that slogan before. I do not think it has meant more to them than it does today. And we recently saw as well their generals bragging that one of our bases is now within reach.

With the minute I have remaining, I wanted to pivot briefly to Iraq because I think it is related to Iran, and it is an interesting dynamic. Obviously, the situation in Syria—not that they were not close already, but the situation in Syria has brought that regime closer and under more of the influence of Iran than ever before, quite frankly dependent on Iran and Russia for their survival. And now we are seeing something similar potentially play out in Iraq where increasingly because of ISIL's gains over the last 72 to 96 hours, we have to assume that the Iranians are all in with regard to pushing back against that. And we know that there was the presence of these Shia militias, many of whom have been equipped and trained, if not all of them, by Iranian forces.

From a regional perspective—and of course, the interesting dynamic is that in many respects we actually share an enemy in ISIL even though our interests may not coincide in terms of the long term. In fact, they do not coincide in terms of the long-term future for that area.

But I wanted your take on what is happening now with regard to Iraq and Malaki and that government's increasing dependence and/or reliance on Iran for potentially its very survival.

Dr. KAGAN. A couple of quick points about Iraq. One is the Iranians, I do not believe, have the capability to help Malaki regain control of his country any more than they have been able to enable Assad to regain control of his country. We continue to have a theoretical opportunity in Iraq because we can offer the Iraqis something that the Iranians cannot. We have both the capability and the desire to help the Iraqis reconquer all of their territory from ISIS, which I believe that we could with the rapid use of military force, which is certainly not going to happen under this administration.

So we are in a situation, as we always have been in Iraq, which is that the Iraqis will take Iranian assistance, especially when there is nothing else on offer, but they would prefer our assistance because we can offer them things that the Iranians cannot.

Another thing that we have to be very clear about, in a certain sense we have been having a fictional conversation here about sanctions. In the real world, unless we are prepared to sanction Iraq, the sanctions regime is unraveling anyway. The Iranians have been working aggressively to expand their ability to export oil and many other things through Iraq. We have turned a blind eye to it. I understand that in the current context. I do not see how we could sanction Malaki while we are trying to help him fight for his life. But what that means is that there is an oil spigot in the Persian Gulf for Iranian oil that we will not be able to control. And as we talk about sanctions, we need to keep that in mind as well.

Ambassador ROSS. Can I make two quick points?

First, I think we should be prepared to help in Iraq, given the stakes, but there should be conditions for Malaki. One of the reasons we are where we are is precisely because the way Malaki has governed, which is to say he has governed in a completely non-inclusive fashion. He has basically alienated the Sunnis in a way that was not required. And if we help, there has to be some change in his behavior in order to do this.

The second point is if we help, it cannot look in the region like—yes, ISIS is a threat to us and to our regional friends, but it cannot look like we are prepared there to help to counter them, but we are not prepared to go against what the Iranians are doing in Syria because then it looks like all we are doing is helping to shift the regional balance more in Iran's favor.

Dr. KAGAN. And I agree with both of those comments.

Mr. MODELL. The only other thing I would add, Senator Rubio, is when you look at the U.S. Government forces that are involved in monitoring the Iran threat network around the world, there are things that we could potentially do to address some of the issues you are talking about, particularly Iran's potential movement to a greater extent into Iraq. I will give you an example.

The Department of the Treasury has done a fantastic job in some senses, but in others, it just does not have the resources to do what it needs to do. So OFAC designations. When you look at the thousands of Iranian entities or individuals and groups who have been designated over the years as violators of sanctions, what has happened as a result of that? They simply close this door and open up another one. There needs to be a comprehensive look at what Treasury's OFAC designations—what the impact of that has been and what gaps we need to address because if you are looking at ways—in the context of the greater nuclear issue, are we going to have a comprehensive long-term verification mechanism that really works? Well, a lot of the cheating that has gone on over the years could have been prevented if we had better overseas capability, quite frankly, not on our own but with liaison partners to actually verify the designations are being honored.

The CHAIRMAN. Senator Flake.

Senator FLAKE. Thank you. I appreciate the testimony.

Ambassador Ross, we are coming up right now at the end of our negotiating period and determining whether we want to extend or not. What concerns are there that if we do not continue, that our allies might leave us behind, figure nothing will ever be good enough for the Americans, we will cut our own deal? Is there a concern about that? Should we be concerned about that? And is that something that motivates us to stay at the table?

Ambassador ROSS. I think the answer is "yes" because I think the other members of the 5+1—precisely because the joint plan of action built into it a renewable 6 months for a total of 1 year by mutual agreement, I am quite certain that all the other members are going to say, look, rather than walking away, let us take the other 6 months and let us see if we can, in fact, reach a comprehensive agreement.

I think beyond, at the end of the next 6 months, we may be in a different place. But a lot depends upon the Iranians. Are they nonresponsive? Do they stay in the position they are right now, which signals they are not close to understanding or recognizing what is being required? They are talking right now about wanting thousands, 30,000, 100,000 centrifuges, not rolling back their program.

Senator FLAKE. Any comment on that, Mr. Kagan? Just to back up a bit, I think we all can see that Iran is at the table because of these sanctions, and it is because that we have had cooperation from our, in particular, European allies on this. And we need them to stay at the table. We need this to be Iran versus the West rather than Iran versus the United States in terms of sanctions. So how much of a motivating factor is that for the United States to stay at the table because we need our allies with us?

Dr. KAGAN. I think Ambassador Ross made a very excellent point, which is that deciding that you want to stay at the table is one thing. Actually getting an agreement to stay at the table and extend is another thing. That technical discussion about what the extension would look like is probably going to be more determinative of whether we can do this than anything else.

I am a little bit less worried at the prospect that if we walk away from the table, the European states will decide the heck with us and do a unilateral deal with Iran. There are a lot of other issues in play. As always, we talk about this in isolation. There is tremendous nervousness about Russia and the threat to NATO in general. There is a tremendous concern about alienating the United States even more to the point where we withdraw entirely at a moment when people seem to need us a great deal. And so I think a lot of calculations would be made regarding whether we actually are going to see European partners just torpedo us entirely. So I am a little less pessimistic about that even though I would be surprised if we ended up walking away.

Senator FLAKE. The concern about extension and going for a full year, obviously, is if Iran is gaming the system now in a way that puts them closer to being a threshold state. Is it your opinion, Mr. Modell or Mr. Ross, that this time period does allow them to get closer? Or are they truly rolling back in a way that benefits us in terms of a final deal?

Mr. MODELL. I would say I think they are already a nuclear threshold state. They have the ability. If they wanted to cross that threshold and to make that move to actually break out, they could do that. I do not necessarily think that they are trying to delay for another 6 or 12 months. I think they honestly want to see if they can actually work their way into a deal that will allow them to pursue an agenda that may not be totally transparent to us right now, particularly on the military dimensions of their program. But they need time to do that. So I do not think it is just simply a matter of buying time.

But I would make a comment too. On the United States corporate side, we have talked to a number of companies, particularly in the energy field, who are like everybody wondering at what point it would be prudent to start taking a serious look about reentering the Iranian market. There is a great deal of reluctance on their part. Really. And it is not only in terms of the sanctions and the political risk involved, but it is simply there are a lot of fundamentals in terms of the deals that will be struck on production-sharing agreements and other forms with the fundamental agreements they would need to have in place rather than to even consider going back in.

Senator FLAKE. Well, I think from what we hear, Iran thought that they might get more out of this interim deal than they actually are in terms of sanctions relief. It has been more difficult just because of the interlocking nature of these sanctions and the reluctance of people to get involved. So that is, frankly, a good sign.

Ambassador ROSS. I do not think, in answer to your question, they are not able to game the system very much, given the nature of this agreement. The one area where they have the potential to game is that they can do R&D on the existing centrifuges that they have. So they cannot deploy any new centrifuges except one of those that break down. But it means that the R&D that they are doing on the existing centrifuges—and they have several generations—means at the end of this, they would be in a better position to move quickly. But the fact is during this time, that is the only area where they are able to do anything that potentially advance them. And the 20 percent they have dismantled. So from that standpoint, they are a little bit farther removed from where their breakout capability might have been prior to the time of the deal.

Dr. KAGAN. I have to disagree with Ambassador Ross on one important point. There is a realm in which they can advance because this agreement has done virtually nothing to improve our ability to detect their pursuit of weaponization technology. And I have long believed that that is actually the long pole in the tent. They clearly have the capability under any scenario to process enough uranium to produce enriched uranium. We are just talking about timelines there.

The challenges that they have been facing have been developing a working nuclear device small enough and reliable enough to put on a reentry vehicle and so forth. There is absolutely nothing in this deal in my opinion that has harmed their ability to continue to pursue that effort in any meaningful way.

Senator FLAKE. Mr. Kagan, I was interested in your contention at the beginning that Iran's nuclear ambitions are secondary to their regional ambitions in other areas. If we were to strike a deal and get a deal that we are comfortable with and comfortable enough to move ahead, what would be our next step—the United States that is—in terms of trying to influence Iran in terms of its regional activities? Would we be in a much better position to have influence on them or not in your view?

Dr. KAGAN. I think it depends on whether or not the administration does what Ambassador Ross is telling them to do. If we were to right now design and implement and execute a strategy to combat Iranian influence around the region, put pressure on the Iranian regime and so forth in pursuit of a good deal, then we could emerge, theoretically, at the end of those negotiations in a better position. If we do not do that and if we do not work to strip away from them the capabilities that they are using to operate in the way that they are throughout the region, then a deal will simply open the flood gates and we will be in a much worse position.

Senator FLAKE. Thank you, Mr. Chairman.

The CHAIRMAN. Senator Paul.

Senator PAUL. Thanks to the panel for coming today.

Since we have had some lessening of the sanctions with the interim agreement with Iran, people talk about them being easily reversible. I am not really so concerned about the technical aspect of being easily reversible, but I am concerned about whether or not the reconstitution of an international coalition, which I think the sanctions, I think everyone would agree, are not as successful if it is just us—I am interested in the panel's opinion on whether or not we have gone beyond getting everybody back together. Is there going to be the ability, if there is no deal or if there is the sense that Iran is evading even the interim deal, to reconstitute an international coalition to make sanctions effective? Where do you think we are in that spectrum of being able to reconstitute that?

Ambassador ROSS. I think the ability to sustain this is much greater when you can point to Iran's bad behaviors. So if in the end, they are not responsive and there has been clearly a serious effort to try to offer them something and they are not responsive, it becomes much easier to sustain this with the kind of collective enforcement that we are seeing.

Mr. MODELL. Senator, I would just add to that. When you look at the task before us and trying to figure out, is bad behavior going to occur in terms of illegal proliferation—illegal actions on the part of the threat network that they have got in the region—one of the things that we have not done a good enough job of, I think, in the U.S. Government, is actually defining what a comprehensive verification and compliance regime needs to look like. It is not that easy simply to say that we are going to crack down on Iran. There are a lot of things that we do not do very well. There are a lot of risks that we are unwilling to take. There is a lot of liaison relationships out there with allied countries, by the way, that do not have the resources they need, that do not have the support they need, and do not have the transparency from us, including Israel I would say. Ambassador Ross made a comment earlier about the need for us to have actually a common understanding with regard to Israel as to what is it going to look like when we jointly try to pursue efforts to figure out if the Iranians are cheating or not. Half the time, we do not know what the Israelis are doing. They do not know what we are doing. There has to be better dialogue and transparency on sensitive regional and global issues if you are going to be serious about trying to figure out if they are cheating or not.

Dr. KAGAN. Senator, if the question is can we reconstitute the regime exactly as it was and continue to strengthen it in the way that we had been doing it; I am not sure. We certainly have the problems with Russia that we have. We have problems with China that we have. So I am not sure we are going to be able to continue to do that.

However, I think that Scott has pointed out quite rightly that as long as we can keep the current resolutions in place and the current agreements in force—and I think that is a perfectly feasible undertaking—we have the ability to improve our own prosecution of the sanctions in a way that can bring additional pain on Iran.

Senator PAUL. One quick followup. All of you who feel like nobody is evading beyond or lessening the sanctions beyond what we sort of agreed to lessen them to—Russia and China and others—they are still adhering to the previous set of sanctions that supposedly are in place?

Dr. KAGAN. No.

Senator PAUL. But you do think they are.

Dr. KAGAN. Absolutely, yes. I am certain that they are and the Iranians are evading the sanctions in a variety of ways, including through Iraq, as I said.

Senator PAUL. And then the only other point I would like to make—and I think this is an important one because I try to think about these as if—you know, what a soldier thinks about our soldier unit that you might send back into Iraq, which I am not very excited about.

We released three Moroccans from Gitmo a while back under the previous administration. They went home for a while and then they decided to go fight in Syria. They are fighting on the same side as we are in Syria. So people who hate America are on our side, which concerns me a bit and confuses me a bit.

We are supporting a Sunni sort of movement. It has people we say we are not going to give weapons to, but we did give some to a military council that said recently that said they are going for the Golan Heights when they are done with Assad. That is confusing to me to be on the same side as people who are going to try to reclaim the Golan Heights.

It is a Sunni resistance. It also has parts of ISIS in it. But now we are sort of supportive of ISIS. Not really, but we are on the same side as ISIS in one battle.

So you tell a GI who is going to carry a gun and put his life down—and I know a guy from my neighboring town lost both legs and an arm, and he fought for freedom. He fought for our Bill of Rights. He fought for our Constitution. But you can see how it might be confusing when you send a soldier back in there that you say, well, Iran supports Hezbollah and the Allawites and the Shiites, but Iran also likes Malaki and the Shiites in there. So you can see how it is very confusing. We are on both sides of two different wars.

To be at war and to kill people and to fight and to lay down your life—it is hard for me to be certain that I am excited to go. I mean, I hate that Mosul is falling and I hate that those are falling, but I also think for 10 years we have supplied the Iraqis. They cannot stand up and do anything to defend their country and it is all up to us? It is hard for me.

And I think it is easy from a geopolitical point of view. All the things you say are rational and logical, but I see this also emotionally from a GI who has to go over there and potentially lose his life, an American. And I am concerned that it is confusing. Which side are we on? We are for the Sunnis in one war, and we are against the same set of Sunnis in another war in a neighboring place. It is all destabilizing.

But you could even go back 10 years and say, you know, what? It might have been a little more stable when we had that awful guy Hussein who hated the Iranians. So I am not saying I am for having Hussein there. I am just saying that geopolitically you had people somewhat at a standstill over there, and now you have a really confusing mess that makes it hard for me or for a GI to understand who he is shooting at and why and he is shooting at one person in one war and a different person in another war, neighboring war.

Ambassador ROSS. Can I make just one quick response to that?

Look, what you are saying is, obviously, a reality. But I think one way to think about it is that there are radical Shia militias who are armed, trained, funded by the Iranians. There is ISIS. These are extremist radical Sunnis. Both are our enemies. Both hate us. Both threaten us. So the key is to identify who are our natural partners who are contending with both, and how do we support them? We have to be able to discriminate enough and then we have to be able to figure out how to do that.

Senator PAUL. But would you agree it is hard to sort of decide who are our friends and who are not? We have given antitank weapons to a group in Syria that 2 weeks ago said that they will attack Israel. And we have already given them weapons. We let three people go from Gitmo who are fighting on the same side of the war. It is confusing. And there are radical elements, but they have hated each other for thousands of years, and they are probably going to hate each other for another thousand years and fight each other.

I am not really saying do not be involved. I am saying try to help in some way, but really think seriously before we say, oh, it is real easy. We have the might. We do. We could go in and we could do it. But are you willing to let 4,000 more soldiers die in Iraq, Americans, to bring back Mosul? I think it is terrible what is happening, but the Iraqis need to step up and defend their country. And I just do not know if I am ready to send 4,000 soldiers in.

I am also disturbed that we still have it on the books that the President, while you say he is unlikely, which I agree—it is still on the books that he could—we could go to war tomorrow with no vote of Congress. This is very, very tragic. And at the very least, even if everybody else disagrees with me and they want to go war in Iraq again, we should vote on it. For goodness sakes, we should not have permanent war that you can just go to war anytime you want. That is the way it exists right now. I am very troubled by that.

And this is not really clear-cut exactly who we are for or who we are against, who we are shooting, and we are shooting different people in different wars. It is quite confusing I think. And for someone who is going to lay down their life, it needs to be much more, I think, clear-cut who is our enemy.

Dr. KAGAN. May I respond to that, please?

Senator, I do not know anyone who is excited about going back to Iraq. I do not know anyone who thinks it will be easy. And I do not know anyone who is advocating it with a light heart or in a way that does not imagine that this is going to be incredibly painful.

Senator PAUL. You are in favor of sending troops back into Iraq now?

Dr. KAGAN. Sir, I am in favor of being prepared to do that rather than allowing an al-Qaeda franchise to establish a full-up state with an army with vehicles stretching from——

Senator PAUL. And I do not question your motives. I mean, I think you are sincere. You are all trying to think this through. We are all Americans. We are always trying to do the right things. So I do not question your motives. But let us be clear. You are for sending troops into Iraq——

Dr. KAGAN. Yes, sir. I am very clear about that.

Senator PAUL. But to do that, you have to be prepared to also say—are you prepared to lose 4,000 lives if it takes it to get Mosul back? And that is a real question. Are you prepared to have 4,000 soldiers more die to take back Iraq again and try for another 10 years? Then what happens in 10 years? Do we have to stay 20, 30, 50? The war has been going on a thousand years.

Ambassador ROSS. Can I just say one thing?

I am not sure the choice is either you have to send troops back in or you do nothing. And I do not think we want to put ourselves in a position where our choice is you have to send troops in or you do nothing. There are options short of that, and we have to think through those because if, in fact, ISIS is able to establish a strong foothold in northern Iraq, we will end up finding that they do not just attack others within the area. It will become a base to attack us.

Senator PAUL. And we will go in as allies of Iran. And I myself am concerned about Iran. I am for the sanctions. I voted for all the sanctions. But if we go to war again in Iraq, we will go to war as allies of Iran. So it is a little bit confusing to tell a soldier you are going over there. We must do everything possible, including war, to keep Iran from having nuclear weapons, and yet we will be allied with Iran in a war in Iraq. It is confusing. It is not clear-cut.

Dr. KAGAN. Senator, I am very confident that our soldiers will be able to understand who the enemy is largely because there will be the enemy that is shooting at them, and they have shown in the past that they can do that. The soldiers we are talking about and officers are my friends. These are the people that I have also served with overseas. I understand the costs of this war, as well as you do, sir. And I understand the risks of sending troops into this conflict, as well as you do.

I would not send American boots on the ground into this conflict in the first instance. I agree with Ambassador Ross. There are things to do short of that.

But I agree with the point that you are making fundamentally, Senator, which is a very important one, that we should not imagine that there is an easy course of action here that is a limited action that is either guaranteed success or that we can do it and then say, well, it did not work and we are done with it. I am saying that if we are going to involve ourselves in this, we should be prepared to——

The CHAIRMAN. I have allowed this to go on for a while, and I know everybody is passionate about their views and I appreciate that. There is a vote that is shortly going to be coming up. So I am sure the debate will continue.

I will say one point about Iraq. It is not the focus of this hearing but elements of it have seeped in. As someone who voted against the war in Iraq, I can tell you that the biggest beneficiary of President Bush's engagement in Iraq has been Iran. And we are facing the flow of consequences from that. And it is not neat and it is not nice.

I do believe after so many lives and national treasure that to do nothing is probably unacceptable in our national interests and our national security. But what that is I think there can be targeted, limited, but significant assistance to the Iraqis but only—and this is where I agree with Ambassador Ross—but only if Malaki is willing to make public statements with reference to a nonsectarian agenda and an Iraqi unity regardless of sector ethnicity, and uses the opportunity to unify his country because we can train all you want.

But when I was in Iraq and I asked are these soldiers really ready to fight for their country or is this a job—Americans when they sign up, especially in a volunteer army, are fighting for their country. They are fighting for a set of principles and beliefs. If it is just a job, there is a whole different set of circumstances. And so unless there is a sense of national unity and purpose, this will never be a successful set of circumstances.

I appreciate this panel's insights. It has been very helpful. There is a lot more work to be done on the Iran question and many dimensions to it. And I am sure we will be engaging with you in the days ahead.

With the appreciation of the committee, this hearing is adjourned.

[Whereupon, at 12 p.m., the hearing was adjourned.]

www.ingramcontent.com/pod-product-compliance
Lightning Source LLC
Chambersburg PA
CBHW080918290526
45795CB00007BA/2561

* 9 7 8 1 5 1 4 2 6 6 9 3 9 *